G.F. QUINN

# Type 2 Diabetes Cookbook for Beginners

*Quick and Easy Mouth-Watering Recipes to Help Manage Type 2 Diabetes: A Better Way to Eat Healthy Without Sacrificing Your Taste Buds!*

*First edition*

*This book was professionally typeset on Reedsy.*
*Find out more at reedsy.com*

# Contents

# 1

# Introduction

I am a type 2 diabetic; my doctor recommended a simple blood test when I was 40 years old, which revealed that I had type 2 diabetes. My parents were both type 2 diabetics; my mother was diagnosed when she was 28, and my father was diagnosed in his mid-40s.

Having said that, nearly everyone on the planet has met or heard of someone with diabetes, perhaps a friend or relative. When you are diagnosed with type 2 diabetes, you must make some lifestyle changes to maintain a healthy life.

I can attest that it hasn't always been simple; there have been many challenges to overcome. I can honestly claim that eating healthy has improved my life.

Going on this life-changing journey might be scary since you are expected to quickly change your eating habits, which can be challenging for people who have recently been diagnosed with type 2 diabetes.

You rapidly realize that if you do not adequately manage your type 2 diabetes, you risk getting heart disease, chronic kidney disease, nerve damage, and other foot, oral, eyesight, hearing, and mental health difficulties.

Throughout this book, I will share detailed diabetes-appropriate recipes that have worked for me over the years, as well as which foods are the best and worst for diabetes. I've included meal planners to help you plan out all of your diabetes meals. I also include a list of dietary food options to help you control type 2 diabetes, as well as guidelines for managing and treating type 2 diabetes.

We'll go through the many types of diabetes, what they are, and what to do if you feel you're suffering from diabetic symptoms.

If you suddenly experience diabetic symptoms or come into contact with someone who does, dial 9-1-1 immediately.

# 2

# What Exactly is Diabetes?

Diabetes mellitus is an illness that affects insulin, a hormone that transforms sugars in food into glucose to fuel the body. It affects around 420 million people worldwide.

Diabetes is a disease in which the body wrongly converts food into energy. The pancreas produces insulin, a crucial chemical that transports glucose (sugar) to your body's cells. Diabetes occurs when your body either does not respond to insulin or does not produce insulin in any way. This causes glucose to accumulate in your blood, putting you at risk of serious problems.

What if I'm unsure whether I have diabetes? What are the negative consequences? I could see from my own firsthand knowledge that something was wrong with me and how I felt. I was constantly thirsty, needing frequent trips to the bathroom; my energy level was low; and I was exhausted all of the time. I was convinced that something was wrong, so I went to see my primary care physician, and after a battery of tests, I was diagnosed with type 2 diabetes.

Because blood sugar levels determine your diabetes symptoms, my diagnosis does not apply to everyone. Some people, particularly prediabetics, gestational diabetics, and type 2 diabetics, may experience no symptoms. Type 1 diabetics, on the other hand, have significantly more severe and immediate symptoms.

While there are many symptoms of type 2 diabetes that can be damaging and even fatal, this is only true if you let your diagnosis control how you live. I stated that if I had what was needed to treat my type 2 diabetes, I would go to any length to obtain it. Even purchasing a book.

Type 2 diabetes is not a death sentence; it can offer challenges, but educating ourselves on how to properly control it with basic meal recipes, workouts, and prescriptions will make life a lot easier. I'm not asking you to spend a lot of money on food since eating well doesn't have to be expensive.

**How do I find out if I have type 2 diabetes?**

I'll concentrate on type 2 diabetes because it is the most common among people. Your doctor will do one of many blood sugar level tests to correctly diagnose type 2 diabetes. Glycated hemoglobin (A1C) Test: My doctor recommended a blood test to determine whether or not I had diabetes. My average blood sugar level over the past two to three months was indicated by this blood test. Type 2 diabetes is indicated by a score of 6.5% or higher.

Random Blood Sugar Test: Testing yourself with a blood glucose meter on a regular basis is a good idea, which I had to get used to. For this test, blood sugar was measured in milligrams of sugar per deciliter of blood (mg/dl). A blood sugar level of 200 mg/dl or higher is indicative of type 2 diabetes, especially if you experience symptoms like excessive thirst and frequent urination.

**Are there any side effects of type 2 diabetes?**

Unfortunately, there are numerous factors that can harm someone with type 2 diabetes. The majority of people have to deal with three major issues: heart disease, chronic renal illness, and nerve damage. In addition, they may experience a variety of foot, mouth, eyesight, hearing, and mental health issues are among them. Please see your doctor to discover how to avoid or delay the effects of diabetes and how to improve your overall health.

People with type 2 diabetes are more likely to develop cardiovascular disease. We have twice the risk of heart disease or stroke as non-diabetics. Over time, high blood sugar levels can damage blood vessels and the nerves that control our hearts.

Type 2 diabetes also increases the risk of high blood pressure, high LDL cholesterol, and high triglycerides, all of which raise the risk of heart disease. If you or someone you know is experiencing symptoms of a heart attack, call 9-1-1 immediately.

Retinopathy (damage to the retina): I visit my optometrist twice a year for a comprehensive eye examination. High blood sugar levels can damage the blood vessels of the retina, cutting off blood flow.

Retinopathy causes 10,000 new cases of blindness each year in the United States alone, and the number is climbing. Diabetes type 2 can lead to more significant vision disorders, such as cataracts and glaucoma.

Nerve damage in the limbs (neuropathy) occurs when high blood sugar levels are sustained for a prolonged amount of time, causing tingling, numbness, burning, pain, or a complete loss of feeling in the toes and fingers.

When the extremities of a person show evidence of discoloration, such as discolored toes or fingers, this is a sure marker of neuropathy. Consult your doctor immediately since, if left untreated, this could lead to serious complications.

A kidney injury is referred to as nephropathy. High hyperglycemia affects the blood vessels in the kidneys that filter waste, resulting in kidney injury.

Diabetes can cause chronic kidney disease or irreversible end-stage kidney failure, necessitating dialysis or a kidney transplant.

If you or someone you know has renal failure, you will notice symptoms of water retention, which are comparable to bloating, particularly on your hands, arms, legs, and feet. You need to see your doctor right away to begin treatment for water retention.

Currently, these issues may not arise spontaneously, but excessive glucose levels can gradually harm a variety of vital systems, including your heart and kidneys, as well as your nerves and veins. You should consult your primary care physician on a regular basis to learn more about how type 2 diabetes affects your overall health, something I do all the time.

**What can I do to keep my type 2 diabetes under control?**

You can take numerous steps to control and maintain your type 2 diabetes. As diabetics, we believe that adopting a healthier lifestyle could have prevented 78% to 83% of new type 2 diabetes cases.

Losing weight: If you are overweight, losing merely 5% of your body weight can help you avoid type 2 diabetes. This equates to a 10-pound weight loss for someone weighing 200 pounds.

Exercise: Moving more helps in the regulation of blood sugar and weight, as well as the reduction of blood pressure and cholesterol, all of which are risk factors for diabetes. You don't even have to work out hard, which is great in my opinion.

According to the National Institutes of Health, 30 minutes of daily walking or other low-intensity exercise paired with a low-fat diet lowers the risk of type 2 diabetes by 58%.

Diet: Reduce your risk of type 2 diabetes by eating as many non-starchy vegetables, fruits, lean meats, other proteins (eggs, beans, lentils, etc.), and whole grains as is affordable. Reduce your intake of processed foods, trans fats, and sugary beverages. Throughout this book, I will go into further detail on the dietary food options recommended for a type 2 diabetic.

By doing these things, you can help delay and control your type 2 diabetes. Consult your doctor(s) and a RD (registered dietitian), who will work with you to create a personalized type 2 diabetes treatment plan and dietary meal plan.

In the following chapter, I will describe the different types of diabetes and how to distinguish them. Each has its own set of challenges, but with the right information, we can successfully manage our diabetes.

# 3

# How Many Types of Diabetes are There?

Most people will tell you that there are only two types. Another, as already mentioned, is gestational diabetes. I'll go over each one in depth.

Gestational diabetes: Every year, gestational diabetes affects up to 10% of pregnancies in the United States. So please know that you are not alone. And keep in mind that this does not imply that you had diabetes prior to conception or that you will have diabetes after delivery. It indicates that you can have a safe pregnancy if you work with your doctor. Whatever happens, you have all the help you need for both you and your baby.

**We have no idea what causes gestational diabetes...**

We do know that hCG (Human chorionic gonadotropin hormone) is only made during pregnancy and is almost exclusively made in the placenta. Hormones can sometimes restrict the effect of insulin on the mother's body resulting in a condition known as insulin resistance. As a result, she may require up to three times the amount of insulin to compensate.

Gestational diabetes can also develop when the mother's body is unable to produce and use all of the insulin required for pregnancy. Glucose cannot leave the circulation and be converted into energy if there is insufficient insulin. Hyperglycemia occurs when glucose levels in the blood rise.

Whatever the cause, you can work with your doctor to develop a plan to ensure a healthy pregnancy and birth. Pose inquiries. Request assistance. There are numerous approaches to combating gestational diabetes.

Type 1: This is the most common in children, with some as young as 5 years old suffering from it. This type simply means that the pancreas does not create any insulin, allowing the immune system to mistakenly destroy the body's own organs or tissues. Because type 1 diabetes symptoms come quickly, most people are unaware that they have diabetes. Type 1 diabetes patients may require many insulin injections per day.

Although there are many similarities between type 1 and type 2 diabetes, both are truly different. In most cases, the treatment is also significantly different. Some patients, especially those newly diagnosed with type 1 diabetes, may have symptoms that are identical to those of type 2 diabetes, which can be perplexing.

**Can type 1 diabetes symptoms appear suddenly?**

Type 1 diabetes symptoms can occur suddenly, whereas type 2 diabetes symptoms may appear gradually, or there can be no symptoms at all.

Symptoms may arise following a viral infection. In some cases, a person may develop diabetic ketoacidosis (DKA) before being diagnosed with type 1 diabetes. DKA happens when blood glucose (blood sugar) levels are dangerously high and the body is unable to deliver nutrients to cells because of an insulin deficiency. The body then uses muscle and fat for energy, causing ketones to accumulate in the blood and urine. A fruity breath odor, heavy, forced breathing, and vomiting are all indications of DKA. If left untreated, DKA can result in stupor, unconsciousness, and even death.

People experiencing symptoms of type 1 diabetes, or DKA, should consult their doctor as soon as possible to receive an accurate diagnosis. Remember that these symptoms could also suggest other problems.

Some people with type 1 diabetes have a "honeymoon" period, which is defined by a brief remission of symptoms while the pancreas continues to generate insulin. The honeymoon period usually occurs after someone starts taking insulin and can last anywhere between a week and a year. It is important to note, however, that the absence of symptoms does not suggest that diabetes is no longer present. If left untreated, the pancreas will eventually be unable to produce insulin, and the symptoms will recur.

Insulin resistance, the primary cause of Type 2 diabetes Insulin resistance affects up to 35.4 million people in the United States alone and is on the rise. Insulin is a pancreatic hormone that is required for delivering glucose (sugar) from the bloodstream to cells throughout our bodies, where it is used for energy. "Insulin resistance" means the cells in our muscles, fat, and liver are not responding well to insulin and are struggling to absorb the glucose from our blood. In Type 2 diabetics, the pancreas increases insulin production in an effort to help glucose enter our cells, but the body resists it, leaving an excess of sugar in the bloodstream.

**What causes type 2 diabetes?**

For many years, there has been a heated discussion concerning what causes type 2 diabetes. There is no single cause of type 2 diabetes that we can identify. A variety of factors or events can contribute to insulin resistance.

Genetics: Type 2 diabetes is more strongly linked to family history and lineage than type 1, and twin studies have shown that genetics play a significant role in the development of type 2 diabetes. Some people, including myself, are genetically prone to insulin resistance and increased insulin production, which leads to type 2 diabetes. As previously stated, people with a family history of diabetes are more likely to develop the disease. Both of my parents had type 2 diabetes.

Obesity: Each year, 30%-53% of new cases of Type 2 diabetes in the United States are caused by obesity. Being overweight or obese may make getting glucose into our cells more challenging, resulting in insulin resistance. Insulin resistance is increased by visceral fat, which surrounds internal organs and causes inflammation throughout our bodies.

Inactivity: When we exercise, our bodies are more receptive to insulin, which means glucose in the blood is transferred more efficiently. Having higher muscle mass also permits our cells to absorb more glucose for energy. We miss out on those benefits when we are inactive, which is defined as not doing anything physical during leisure time for the previous month. Inactivity increases our risk for insulin resistance.

Age: The majority of type 2 diabetes patients are over 45 years old. This is most likely related to the fact that, as we get older, we lose muscle mass and gain fat. These are two of the most important factors influencing insulin resistance, or Type 2 diabetes.

Men are more likely than women to develop type 2 diabetes (14.6% of men have it, compared to 9.1% of women in the United States). This is most likely because, as men age, we develop more visceral fat in our tummies, which is a risk factor.

Diabetes has been shown to disproportionately affect people living in low-income areas, resulting in a lack of basic access to things like healthcare, nutritious food, and safe exercise facilities.

Socioeconomic status differences have been proven in studies to apply to marginalized racial and ethnic populations such as African Americans, Alaska Natives, American Indians, Asian Americans, Hispanics and Latinx, Native

Hawaiians, and Pacific Islanders. Unfortunately, due to factors such as restricted access to healthcare and higher levels of stress, these people are more likely to develop type 2 diabetes.

**What are the symptoms of type 2 diabetes?**

The most common symptoms of type 2 diabetes usually arise gradually. In fact, you could have type 2 diabetes for years without even knowing it. When there are signs and symptoms, they may include the following:

- Increased thirst
- Needing to urinate more frequently
- Increased hunger
- Unknown cause of weight loss
- Fatigue
- Blurry vision
- Sores that heal slowly
- Frequent infections
- Numbness or tingling in your hands or feet
- Developing darkish skin patches, usually in the armpits and neck

Now that we have covered the three most common types of diabetes and what the symptoms are, we can move on to learning steps to prevent and control type 2 diabetes.

Later chapters will include recipes that have worked well for me and that I focus on including into my everyday routine. This was difficult during the pandemic because many of us were told to stay indoors. Having said that, I am able to say that I am a COVID-19 survivor. I spent the majority of the winter of 2020 in the hospital and feel fortunate to have walked out of there.

# 4

# Steps to Prevent and Control Type 2 Diabetes

I wish there was a switch in the back of my skull that could just turn off having type 2 diabetes, but since there isn't, I'll go through some of the actions you can take to help regulate and delay the effects of being diagnosed with type 2 diabetes.

Keeping yourself healthy and eating the right foods may undoubtedly lower your blood sugar levels; however, monitoring your levels is critical. Check with your doctor on what type of glucometer (blood sugar meter) would likely work best for you

Eating a good, fruit-and-vegetable-rich diet, maintaining a healthy weight, and engaging in regular physical activity can all help. Monitor your blood sugar levels (glucometer) to determine what is causing them to rise or fall. Eat at regular intervals, and try not to skip meals.

By practicing these things, you will significantly enhance your lifestyle, feel better and stronger, and have a higher sense of general well-being. Some of the modifications that will be beneficial are listed below.

**What diabetics should read on a food label**

It took me a bit to figure out what I should be looking for, but here's what I've learned over the years. The amount of total fat, saturated fat, trans fat, cholesterol, sodium, total carbohydrate, dietary fiber, carbs, protein, vitamin D, calcium, iron, and potassium in one serving must be specified on the label.

**What are carbohydrates?**

Carbohydrates are sugar molecules that are one of the three fundamental nutrients found in meals and beverages, along with proteins and lipids (fats). Our bodies convert carbs into glucose, also known as blood sugar, which is the primary energy source for our body's cells, tissues, and organs.

Knowing your carbs: Contrary to popular belief, carbohydrates are much more than simply pasta and bread. Carbohydrates are found in all foods that contain starch, including sweets, fruit, milk, and even yogurt. Getting into the habit of counting carbs is a great idea.

**How many carbs can I have?**

They now make it simple to count carbs. To begin, look for the "Total Carbohydrate" statistic on a package's "Nutrition Facts" panel. Then, look at the portion size and confirm how much you can consume. Repeat with the other dishes you intend to eat. When you tally up all of the carbs, the total should be within your meal limit.

Most type 2 diabetics aim for 45 to 60 grams of carbs per meal and 15 to 20 grams of carbs per snack. That figure may change depending on how active you are and the medications you take, so check with your doctor or a registered dietitian (RD).

This is precisely what I did after consulting with a licensed nutritionist. She assisted me in determining the quantity of carbs, protein, and fat I can have at meals and snacks throughout the day to maintain my blood sugar levels (which I check with my glucometer).

**Make healthy lifestyle choices.**

Counting carbs focuses on the number of carbs consumed at each meal rather than the type. Nonetheless, it is advised to choose healthy options wherever possible. Foods and beverages with added sugar are frequently rich in calories and lacking in nutrients. Eating whole grains, fruits, and vegetables can provide you with energy as well as the vitamins, minerals, and fiber that can help you regulate your type 2 diabetes and weight.

**What foods should I start with?**

Eating healthier need not feel overwhelming; start with these small changes.

- Vegetables and fruit: Eat an abundance every day, and be sure to count the carbs.
- Sodium (salt): For many of us, we like the taste of salt in our food. I'm definitely not saying to avoid it all together, but limit yourself to less than 2300 milligrams per day.
- Fish: I like this one, as fish is one of my favorites. It is a good idea to eat fish about 2 to 3 times a week.
- Whole grains: Using whole grains in moderation has been known to help control type 2 diabetes. Remember to count the carbs.
- Sugar: Limit foods with excess sugar, such as desserts, sodas, etc. While sugar itself does not cause diabetes, it is well known that an excess of sugar leads to increased fat storage (weight gain) which can then lead to insulin resistance and Type 2 diabetes.

**Do I drink lots of water?**

When I was originally diagnosed with type 2 diabetes, I believed I had to avoid drinking water, but that wasn't the case. I've discovered that drinking water can help our body get rid of extra glucose (sugar) as well as battle dehydration.

**How much water should I drink each day?**

If you have type 2 diabetes, like me, you should drink around 1.6 liters (L) or 6.5 cups per day for women, and 2 L or 8.5 glasses per day for men.

**Should I quit smoking?**

According to new research, smoking is one of the causes of type 2 diabetes. In fact, those who smoke cigarettes are 30% to 40% more likely than nonsmokers to acquire type 2 diabetes. Smokers with type 2 diabetes are more likely than nonsmokers to struggle with insulin administration and controlling their illness.

Tobacco use on a regular basis can raise our blood glucose (sugar) levels and limit our bodies' ability to use insulin, making it more difficult to regulate our type 2 diabetes. Even a single cigarette, e-cigarette, or small amount of chewing tobacco is dangerous.

**Can a person with type 2 diabetes drink coffee or tea?**

According to a recent study, type 2 diabetics who consume more coffee, tea, or plain water may have a 25% lower risk of dying prematurely from any cause. If you have type 2 diabetes, it's vital to keep your beverages sugar-free, to stick to mainstream green, herbal, or black teas, and to check when you should cut back on caffeine intake to help you sleep better.

**Processed Foods**

According to studies, processed foods' high sugar content may contribute to insulin resistance, diabetes, and high cholesterol levels. Processed foods are especially dangerous for people with Type 1 or Type 2 diabetes since they can significantly raise blood sugar levels.

Processed foods are high in sugar, preservatives, salt, and fat; these foods are bad for everyone, especially people with type 2 diabetes. Remove them from your shopping list to benefit your health.

The United States consumes the most packaged and processed foods per person than any other country. Processed foods are indisputably cheap and handy, but if you have type 2 diabetes, processed foods should be avoided whenever possible.

The issue with eating processed meals is that we are so accustomed to eating them that we rely heavily on them when we are hungry. According to a recent study, the foods listed below should be avoided because they contribute to type 2 diabetes.

Chicken nuggets: These finger foods dip well and satisfy hunger, but grilled chicken strips or a skinless breast are preferable options. Chicken nuggets, whether purchased at a restaurant or from the freezer area, are made with thick breading, which you may forget to count against your daily carbs, and normally contain more salt, oil, and preservatives than anyone needs.

White rice: While it is affordable and simple to prepare, white rice contains fewer nutrients than other versions. If you enjoy rice and want to improve your type 2 diabetes control, try wild or brown rice, barley, bulgur, and quinoa. They take a bit longer to prepare and are more expensive, but they are considerably more healthy and delicious.

White bread and pasta: Like white rice, these foods have been stripped of nutrients during processing and are usually carbohydrate-laden. Instead choose whole grain breads, pastas, or cereals

French Fries: Few people, including me, realize how many calories french fries contain, even in a tiny portion. This can make it harder to control your weight and type 2 diabetes, especially if you eat them frequently. And, like white rice, they don't provide much in return for their blood sugar-lowering effects.

If you really want fries, bake them without oil at home. Better yet, cut sweet potatoes into wedges and bake them. (One of the best types of potato for diabetics, sweet potatoes contain more fiber than white potatoes which helps to lighten the carb load.) Avoid the frozen foods section of your local supermarket, which has a wide variety of 'fries' or other frozen potatoes, and these usually contain oils and preservatives

Canned fruit and vegetables: While eating more fruits and vegetables is recommended, and fresh produce is always more nutrient-rich, 'fresh' is not always possible due to expense, seasonal offerings, supply shortages, etc. So, the next best choice for nutritional value is frozen, then canned.

As for canned goods, if you do not read the labels carefully, you may wind up with fruit that has been canned in a heavy, sugary syrup (fruit canned in its own juice is preferred), or highly salted vegetables. You can minimize the sugar and salt of canned goods by draining and rinsing the contents.

However, if you do not carefully read labels, you may wind up with fruit that has been canned in heavy, sugary syrup. You can minimize the sugar content of these processed meals by draining and rinsing the fruit, but canned fruit in its own juice is preferable to canned fruit in syrup.

Potato chips & fried foods: As a kid, this was one of my favorite snacks. I sense most of us are guilty of snacking on potato chips now and then. However, for people who are trying to lose weight, as many people with type 2 diabetes must, potato chips and other fried foods can swiftly undermine their diet efforts. These processed foods increase your calorie, salt, and preservative intake while delivering little nourishment or fiber, which can impede digestion. (For a quick snack, have a bowl of fruit on the counter. Alternatively, have some crunchy veggie sticks, such as celery or zucchini, with hummus

These processed foods increase your calorie, salt, and preservative intake while delivering little nourishment or fiber, which can impede digestion. For a quick snack, have a bowl of fruit on the counter. Alternatively, serve some veggie sticks with hummus, such as celery or zucchini.

Soda: Drinking a lot of regular soda is usually associated with a type 2 diabetes diagnosis. To better control weight and type 2 diabetes most people convert to artificially sweetened* and/or sugar-free drinks, avoiding sugary drinks entirely. If you like the carbonation of soda, try club soda or sparkling water flavored with lemon or lime juice.

*Be aware that 'diet soda' has actually been linked to weight gain and metabolic syndrome (a group of conditions that occur together, increasing your risk of type 2 diabetes, as well as heart disease and stroke). Some sweeteners in diet soda can cause insulin spikes and ultimately raise blood sugar levels.

Sugary foods: Of course, processed, packaged foods, such as cookies and snack cakes, have a lot of added sugars. But you may not be aware that common foods such as sweet pickle relish, ketchup, jams and jellies, and salad dressings, have added sugars.

The American Heart Association suggests that you limit your daily intake of added sugars to no more than 6 teaspoons (tsp), or 25 grams (g), for women, and 9 teaspoons (tsp), or 36 grams (g) for men. Check food labels for added sugars like high fructose corn syrup, molasses, honey, or fruit juice concentrates. To better manage your type 2 diabetes, try developing a taste for fewer sweet foods.

Processed meats: Although processed meats do not often include sugar, they are higher in fat and high in salt and preservatives. Consuming processed meats has been linked to an elevated risk of type 2 diabetes. Instead of using lunch meats, deli meats, and various kinds of sausages, choose a leaner cut of meat that is closer to its natural state. Lunchbox sandwiches are best made using leftovers from roasted chicken. Include more meatless options, as well, to help you regulate your type 2 diabetes.

Fast food hamburgers: This fast food staple may put you at risk for diabetes. A study published in the American Journal of Clinical Nutrition in February 2010 found that African American women who eat hamburgers at least twice a week are substantially more likely to be diagnosed with type 2 diabetes than those who do not.

A modest, simple hamburger is unlikely to be the crux of the problem; rather, it is the enormous patties, buns, and toppings that are contributing to these figures. If you're going out to eat, go for a small grilled chicken sandwich with loads of veggies. It is advised to plan nutritious meals ahead of time by researching restaurant menus using apps such as MyFitnessPal, Nutritionix, or CalorieKing.

Cereals with added sugar: Brightly colored breakfast cereal boxes are a staple in many households. You are correct in assuming that added sugar is part of the difficulty that these processed foods provide for those who are type 2 diabetics. The other issue is a lack of dietary fiber, which has been demonstrated to help both prevent and manage type 2 diabetes. It is best to seek out cereals that include at least 5 g of fiber and less than 7 g of sugar per serving.

**How much fiber can I eat?**

For people who are type 2 diabetics, the recommended dietary fiber consumption ranges from 30 to 50 grams per day, with less than a third coming from soluble fiber. Fiber has a number of advantages for diabetics, including that it slows carbohydrate absorption, causing blood sugar levels to rise less after a meal.

Furthermore, the American Diabetes Association (ADA) recommends that people who are type 2 diabetics consume at least 14 grams of fiber per 1,000 calories per day, which is the level recommended in the Dietary Guidelines for Americans (DGA).

**Is there any benefit for a diabetic to take a multivitamin?**

The American Diabetes Association's Standards of Medical Care state that taking a multivitamin provides no significant benefits to those with diabetes as compared to people without diabetes. Diabetes patients can take any supplement or vitamin that is recommended for the general public.

It's not that diabetic patients have low vitamin absorption. Vitamins simply help diabetics supplement their diet, especially if they struggle to consume enough fruits and vegetables, and vitamins are essential to living a healthy life if you have a chronic condition like diabetes.

Always consult your doctor, who can requisition blood tests to see if you have any vitamin deficiencies. Working together, your doctor can recommend the ideal supplementation for you and your lifestyle.

People who take metformin for type 2 diabetes may have reduced vitamin B12 levels. If you're using metformin, talk to your doctor about having regular B12 deficiency tests.

**How much and how often should I exercise?**

The American Diabetes Association recommends at least 150 minutes of moderate-to-high-intensity physical exercise each week and two to three bouts of resistance training per week. Include activities that train all main muscle groups (legs, hips, back, belly, chest, shoulders, and arms) on two or more days each week.

If a semi-intense workout isn't your style, go for a casual stroll around the neighborhood. In fact, studies have shown that exercising for 10 minutes after meals reduces blood sugar by 22%.

**Medications**

There are a number of medications available to treat Type 1 and Type 2 diabetes. The kind you receive will depend on your diagnosis, health, and other factors. Insulin is the number one treatment for Type 1 diabetes. However, the focus of this book is type 2 diabetes, so I will share the most common medications for the treatment of type 2.

Insulin: The hormone insulin is made in the pancreas. It allows the body to use glucose for energy. Type 2 diabetes occurs when the body doesn't use insulin properly (e.g. insulin sensitivity/insulin resistance), thus allowing too much glucose to remain in the blood stream. There are more than 20 varieties of insulin available in the United States. They differ in terms of how quickly they begin working, how long they work, and whether or not they have a peak level of effectiveness. The degree of insulin shortage and insulin sensitivity determine the type of insulin you will need. It is administered as an infusion beneath the skin (using an insulin pump) or as an injection.

Metformin: The liver manufactures and stores glucose depending upon the body's need. Metformin works by reducing the amount of glucose produced by the liver, as well as the amount of glucose absorbed by your intestines. It also assists your muscles in absorbing glucose and makes your body more responsive to insulin. Metformin has been in use for over 30 years and is the most frequently prescribed oral medication for the treatment of Type 2 diabetes.

Insulin and metformin are the two most commonly prescribed medications for type 2 diabetes. More recently other drugs, such as Ozempic injectable and Rybelsus tablets, are being prescribed as 'stand-alone' medications or in combination with others. Additional drugs are continually being evaluated and, once approved, are introduced and prescribed for the treatment of type 2 diabetes. Consult with your doctor to determine which medication(s) are best suited to your specific needs.

**Talk with a doctor**

There are numerous drugs available to treat type 1 and type 2 diabetes. They each help you control your blood sugar in different ways.

Remember to consult with your doctor to determine which type 2 diabetic medication is best for you. They will provide suggestions depending on your diabetes type, health, and other considerations. It's also crucial to note that new diabetic treatments are continually being evaluated for approval.

To recap, taking these actions can improve your quality of life and help you better control and manage your type 2 diabetes. To assist you further, I will discuss the dietary food options that are recommended for a type 2 diabetic.

# 5

# Dietary Food Options for a Type 2 Diabetic

There is so much information out there on what foods are good and bad for type 2 diabetics, but figuring out what you can and can't eat might be difficult. Food choices are highly important when you have type 2 diabetes. Naturally, some are better than others.

Nothing is completely off-limits. Even foods you might consider "the worst" can be eaten in moderation as an occasional treat. Just remember that it is much easier to control Type 2 diabetes if you stick to "the best" nutritional options available

**Best nutritional options for type 2 diabetics**

Green leafy vegetables: I aim to eat these on a daily basis because they are incredibly healthy and low in calories. Spinach, kale, and other leafy greens are high in nutrients, providing a variety of vitamins and minerals, including vitamin C. They also contain antioxidants that protect your heart and eyes

There is some indication that people with type 2 diabetes have lower vitamin C levels than people without diabetes and may require more vitamin C.

24

Increased consumption of vitamin C-rich foods can help people with type 2 diabetes raise serum vitamin C levels while decreasing inflammation and cellular damage.

Fatty Fish: Salmon is one of my favorite foods because it provides omega3 fats, which can assist in lowering inflammation as well as other risk factors for heart disease and stroke. Salmon, sardines, herring, anchovies, and mackerel are all high in protein, which is necessary for blood sugar regulation.

They are also excellent sources of the omega-3 fatty acids DHA and EPA which have considerable cardiovascular benefits. Studies have shown that diabetics who eat fatty fish frequently have a lower risk of acute coronary syndromes such as heart attacks, and are less likely to die from heart disease.

Eggs: I love having eggs for breakfast because there are so many different ways to prepare them. Furthermore, eating eggs on a daily basis may reduce your risk of heart disease in a number of ways.

They have the potential to reduce inflammation, improve insulin sensitivity, increase HDL (good) cholesterol levels, and alter the size and shape of LDL (bad) cholesterol. A high-fat, low-carb breakfast of eggs, according to a 2019 study, may assist persons with type 2 diabetes manage their blood sugar levels throughout the day.

How many eggs should a diabetic eat per day? A controlled trial found that eating 6 to 12 eggs per week as part of a balanced diet did not increase heart disease risk factors in persons with type 2 diabetes.

Avocados: I wasn't a fan at first, but I've come to like nibbling on them over the years because they have less than one gram of sugar and are associated with better overall diet quality. Avocados may potentially have diabetes-prevention qualities.

A mouse study published in 2019 discovered that avocatin B (AvoB), a lipid molecule found solely in avocados, inhibits incomplete oxidation in skeletal muscle and the pancreas, thereby decreasing insulin resistance. Avocados are also considered a 'healthy fat', making them a perfect food for those with type 2 diabetes.

Beans: I believe most of us have eaten some type of bean at one point in our lives. And why not? They are inexpensive to purchase, nourishing, and incredibly healthful. Beans are a type of legume rich in B vitamins and minerals such as calcium, potassium, magnesium, and fiber. In a study of almost 3,000 people at high risk of cardiovascular disease, those who ingested more beans had a lower risk of developing type 2 diabetes.

Chia Seeds: What exactly are chia seeds? I had no idea what they were or where they came from, but they are the edible seeds of Salvia hispanica, a mint family blooming plant endemic to central and southern Mexico, or the similar Salvia columbariae of the southwestern United States and Mexico. Chia seeds are oval and gray in color, with black and white dots, and have a diameter of about 2 millimeters.

Chia seeds are an excellent dietary addition for people with type 2 diabetes as they are very high in fiber and low in digestible carbs, so do not raise blood sugar levels. In fact, fiber accounts for 11 of the 12 grams of carbs in a 28-gram (1-ounce) serving of chia seeds. A study of 77 people with type 2 diabetes who were overweight or obese revealed that eating chia seeds helped them lose weight and maintain good glycemic control.

Broccoli: As far as vegetables go, this is my absolute favorite. It is also one of the most nutrient-dense veggies. A half cup of cooked broccoli contains only 27 calories and 3 grams of digestible carbs, as well as vitamins C and magnesium.

According to one study, eating broccoli sprouts reduced blood glucose levels in people with type 2 diabetes. Finally, broccoli is a low-calorie, low-carbohydrate food that is strong in nutritional value. It is high in beneficial plant components that may help protect against a variety of ailments.

Nuts: These are one of my favorite foods because they are both tasty and healthy. Studies on a variety of nuts have discovered that consuming nuts on a daily basis may reduce inflammation and lower blood sugar, HbA1c (a long-term blood sugar management metric), and LDL (bad) cholesterol levels.

A 2019 study of almost 16,000 adults with type 2 diabetes found that eating tree nuts such as walnuts, almonds, hazelnuts, and pistachios lowered their risk of heart disease and death. They are also a great source of fiber and 'healthy' fats. Overall, eating nuts (in moderation) is a beneficial addition to a well-balanced diet.

Flax Seeds: Flax seeds have been demonstrated to help reduce inflammation, lower the risk of heart disease, lower blood sugar levels, and increase insulin sensitivity. Flax seeds, often known as linseeds or common flax, are high in omega-3 fatty acids, fiber, and other unique plant elements.

One 2016 study of pre-diabetic subjects determined that daily consumption of flax seed powder did not enhance glycemic control or insulin resistance. However, additional research is needed to determine how flax seed can aid in the prevention or management of diabetes. We do know that flax seed is incredibly healthy for your heart and digestive health in general.

Extra Virgin Olive Oil: When determining which olive oil to buy, look for extra virgin olive oil from a reputable seller, as many olive oils are blended with cheaper oils like maize and soy. Oleic acid, a monounsaturated lipid found in extra virgin olive oil, may aid in glycemic control, lower fasting and post-meal triglyceride levels, and have antioxidant properties.

This is significant since people with type 2 diabetes often have difficulty maintaining blood sugar levels and have high triglyceride levels. To further understand the benefits of olive oil, a large analysis of 32 studies looking at different forms of fat found that olive oil was the only one that reduced the risk of heart disease.

Strawberries: Who doesn't enjoy eating fresh strawberries? Strawberries are high in antioxidants known as anthocyanins, which give them their red color. According to a 2017 study, ingesting polyphenols from strawberries and cranberries for 6 weeks improved insulin sensitivity in patients who were overweight or obese but did not have diabetes.

A cup of strawberries contains around 53.1 calories and 12.7 grams of carbohydrates, of which three are fiber. This meal alone provides more than 100% of the RDA for vitamin C, providing additional anti-inflammatory benefits for our cardiovascular health.

Apple Cider Vinegar: Studies have shown that apple cider vinegar improved fasting blood sugar levels in people with Type 2 diabetes, so I've added this to my dietary regimen in recent years. Apple cider vinegar is created when the sugar in apples is fermented to produce acetic acid. Each tablespoon has less than 1 gram of carbohydrates.

How much do I drink? It is suggested that you begin with 4 teaspoons in a glass of water before each meal. You may choose to use 1 teaspoon per glass of water to reduce the intensity of the flavor. Gradually increase the amount to a maximum of 4 tablespoons per day. (Caution: Do not drink apple cider vinegar straight as it can damage the esophagus. Always dilute in water or another liquid.

Squash: This vegetable has long been regarded as one of the healthiest, and it comes in a plethora of variations. Squash, like most vegetables, is high in antioxidants. It also contains less sugar than sweet potatoes, making it an excellent substitute.

Recent research has revealed that pumpkin polysaccharides, which are also contained in squash, improve insulin tolerance and lower serum glucose levels in rats. More human research is needed to show squash's overall health advantages. However, the health benefits of eating squash make it an excellent accompaniment to any meal.

Garlic: Despite its small size, garlic is high in nutrients and low in calories. One clove (3 grams) of raw garlic contains 2% of the daily value (DV). 1% of the DV for vitamin B6, 1% for vitamin C, 1% for selenium, and provides 0.06 grams of fiber. Garlic has been shown in trials to aid with blood glucose control and cholesterol lowering.]

Shirataki Noodles: The starchy, tuberous konjac yam (or elephant yam) is native to Japan where it is farmed and processed into noodles or 'rice' known as Shirataki. These noodles are high in glucomannan (a type of starchy fiber) which recent research has shown dramatically lowers fasting blood glucose, serum insulin, and cholesterol levels in diabetic rats.

This form of fiber, also known as viscous fiber, creates the sensation of feeling full and satisfied. Shirataki noodles provide only 3 grams of digestible carbs and 10 calories for every 3.5-ounce (100-gram) serving, making it an excellent choice for diabetics looking to lose or maintain weight.

If you decide to try these noodles, it is recommended that you rinse them thoroughly before eating because they have a strong, fishy odor. They have almost no flavor on their own, but will take on the flavor of whatever you cook with it. To make them noodle-like, cook the noodles in a skillet over high heat for several minutes without adding fat.]

**The worst food choices that a type 2 diabetic should avoid**

Most individuals with Type 2 diabetes struggle with appropriate food choices. I was one of them, and it took me a long time to realize the significance of eating a healthy diet. The fact that there are so many fast food options available to us doesn't make it any easier. The following foods can have a harmful impact on our cardiovascular health and/or lead to weight gain.

Beverages With Added Sugar: It should come as no surprise to many people that beverages with added sugar, such as soda, sweet tea, and energy drinks, are devoid of essential nutrients. They also contain a large quantity of sugar in each serving, which can cause blood sugar levels to surge.

Refined Grains and Flours: Understanding what refined grains and flours are can be difficult for many of us. White rice and the flours used to make white bread and white pasta are heavy in carbohydrates but lacking in fiber (the bran and fiber are eliminated or greatly reduced during processing). These foods can cause blood sugar levels to rise faster than whole grain options.

Basically, anything "white" made from refined grains is particularly detrimental to people with Type 2 diabetes. Whole grains are the better choice because, according to one study, whole grain rice (like brown rice) was much more effective than white rice at stabilizing blood sugar levels after eating.

Alcohol: People with type 2 diabetes should reduce their alcohol consumption or eliminate intake altogether. This is because alcohol has been linked to an increased risk of low blood sugar, especially when consumed on an empty stomach.

Fried Foods: Most of us have had fried food at some point in our lives. Unfortunately, fried foods (especially those that are deep-fried) include a lot of trans fat, a form of fat that has been linked to an elevated risk of heart disease. More specifically, fried foods such as potato chips, french fries, and mozzarella sticks are often high in calories, leading to weight gain in people with type 2 diabetes.

Candies: It practically goes without saying, but I'll say it anyway: each serving of sweets contains a lot of sugar. It often has a high glycemic index, which means it is extremely likely to trigger blood sugar spikes and falls after eating. Please keep your diabetic medication on hand in case your blood glucose levels fluctuate.

Breakfast Cereal: Most breakfast cereals have a lot of added sugar. Some brands have as much sugar in a single serving as desserts. Because there are so many different types of breakfast cereals available, the best thing you can do for yourself is carefully read the nutritional information and choose a low-sugar variation. Or consider eating cooked oats - the whole oat groat or steel cut - naturally sweetening it by adding a slice of fresh fruit or a few berries.

Fruit juice: Drinking juice isn't always a negative thing, but it should be done in moderation and with caution as it can cause rapid spikes in blood sugar. It is best to consume whole fruits whenever possible, especially if you have type 2 diabetes. 100% fruit juice can be consumed on occasion, but again - with caution - as juice contains all of the carbs and sugars found in fresh fruit but it lacks the fiber required to help balance blood sugar levels.

Processed Meats: As mentioned before, processed meats such as bacon, hot dogs, salami, and cold cuts, are high in sodium (salt), preservatives (such as nitrates and nitrites), and other potentially hazardous ingredients. Many of them are also heavy with trans fats which are related to an increased risk of heart disease.

All fats are classified into four types: saturated, trans, monounsaturated, and polyunsaturated. According to the American Diabetes Association, we should eat more monounsaturated and polyunsaturated fats in our diet rather than saturated or trans fats. Some fats are included on the nutrition facts label; always read the label.]

This knowledge of 'best' and 'worst' food choices may be helpful in managing your blood sugar levels, but the most important thing a person with type 2 diabetes can do for themselves is to eat a nutritious, balanced diet. Doing so will help control blood sugar, insulin, and inflammation which will greatly reduce the risk of complications from diabetes.

In the following pages, I'll share diabetic-friendly recipes and provide some meal planners which will be especially useful for those recently diagnosed with diabetes. I will try not to bore you with too many details because the recipes are self-explanatory with regard to preparation. I apologize to those who want to see pictures of the meals, but there are simply too many recipes to share; added photos would increase the size of this cookbook to around 1,000 pages.

Anyway, let's get this party started, shall we?

# 6

# Breakfast Recipes

Most people start their days with breakfast, but what can a type 2 diabetic have for breakfast? There is virtually an infinite variety available. Below are some of my favorite dishes in full detail. This is by no means a comprehensive list because there is so much a type 2 diabetic can do to enjoy a heart-healthy breakfast. These are just some of my favorites. Mix and match as needed. Enjoy!

**No. 1: Muffin Tin Omelets with Broccoli, Ham, and Cheddar**

It is one of my favorite recipes to cook; there is enough in one dish to last you a full week, and it is ideal for individuals who have an extremely hectic morning.

**Preparation Time:** 20 Minutes

**Extra Time:** 25 Minutes

**Overall Time:** 45 Minutes

**Portions:** 6

**Produced:** 12 Omelets

**Ingredients:**

- Eight large eggs
- 1/2 cup low-fat milk
- 1/4 teaspoon each of salt and ground pepper
- Ham and broccoli, each cut into three-quarter cups
- 6 tablespoons of cheddar cheese, shredded
- 1/4 cup freshly chopped chives

**Directions:**

1. Set the oven's temperature to 325 F.
2. In a big bowl, stir together the eggs, milk, salt, and pepper.
3. Cooking spray or silicone muffin cups should be liberally applied to a 12-cup muffin tray.
4. In the muffin cups, distribute the ham, broccoli, cheddar, and chives.
5. Add the egg mixture on top.
6. Bake for 20 to 25 minutes, or until firm and gently browned. 5 minutes should pass before removing the pan.

**Nutritional Information:** (Per Serving)
164 Calories
10 grams of fat
2 grams of carbs
15 grams of protein

**Nutritional Profile:**
Diabetes-appropriate, gluten-free, high protein, low carbohydrate, nut-free, and soy-free.

**Tips:**

If you are like me and have too many leftovers, just cool them completely and refrigerate them. You can freeze them for up to a month or store them in an airtight jar for up to 3 days. Simply wrap in a paper towel and reheat in the microwave for 30 to 60 seconds on high.

**No. 2: Flourless Banana Chocolate Chip Mini Muffins**

These delightful two-bite muffins have a sweet and gooey feel; baking them as mini muffins is a terrific idea. Ideal for those of us who need a quick breakfast in the morning.

**Preparation Time:** 20 Minutes

**Extra Time:** 30 Minutes

**Overall Time:** 50 Minutes

**Portions:** 24

**Produced:** 24 Muffins

**Ingredients:**

- Rolling oats, 1-1/2 cups (see advice below)
- Baking powder, 1 teaspoon
- Baking soda, 1/4 teaspoon
- Salt, 1/4 teaspoon, and two large eggs
- 1 cup of mashed ripe bananas (about two medium-sized ones)
- 1/3 cup brown sugar in bags
- Canola oil, 3 tablespoons
- Vanilla extract, 1 teaspoon
- 1/2 cup chocolate chips, miniature

**Equipment:** 24-cup mini muffin tin

**Directions:**

1. Set the oven to 350 degrees Fahrenheit.
2. Spray some cooking oil in a 24-cup mini muffin pan.
3. In a blender, pulse oats until they are powdered.
4. Salt, baking soda, and baking powder should be added; pulse once or twice to combine.
5. Blend till smooth after adding the eggs, banana, brown sugar, oil, and vanilla.
6. Add chocolate chunks and stir.
7. Fill the muffin tins as directed.
8. Bake for 15 to 17 minutes, or until a toothpick inserted in the center comes out clean.
9. After 5 minutes on a wire rack in the pan, turn it out to finish cooling.

**Nutritional Information:** (Per Serving)
78 Calories
4 grams of fat
11 grams of carbs
1 gram of protein

**Nutritional Profile:**
Diabetes-appropriate, gluten-free, heart-healthy, low carbohydrate, low sodium, low calorie, nut-free, soy-free, vegetarian.

**Tips:**

There are type 2 diabetics who have celiac disease or a gluten sensitivity; for these reasons, it is recommended that they consume oats labeled "gluten-free," as oats are frequently cross-contaminated with wheat and barley.

## No. 3: Pineapple Grapefruit Detox Smoothie

These components, pineapple, grapefruit, and spinach, are high in water and minerals, which can help hydrate you while also providing your body with a lot of fiber. To make this dairy-free, replace the yogurt or milk with coconut water, a refreshingly rich electrolyte.

**Preparation Time:** 10 Minutes

**Overall Time:** 10 Minutes

**Portions:** 2

**Produced:** 3 Cups

**Ingredients:**

- 1 cup of plain coconut water
- 1 cup of frozen pineapple diced
- 1 cup of packed baby spinach
- 1 small grapefruit, peeled and cut into segments, including any membrane juice
- 1/2 teaspoon freshly grated ginger
- 1 cup of ice

**Directions:**

1. Combine coconut water, pineapple, spinach, grapefruit, any juices, ginger, and ice in a blender.
2. Puree until smooth and frothy. Nothing to it; enjoy!

**Nutritional Information:** (Per Serving)
102 Calories

0 grams of fat

25 grams of carbs

2 grams of protein

## Nutritional Profile:

Diabetes-appropriate, dairy-free, gluten-free, healthy immunity, heart-healthy, low fat, low sodium, low calorie, nut-free, soy-free, vegan, vegetarian

## No. 4: Strawberry-Pineapple Smoothie

In today's day and age, having something readily available is a stress reliever. This strawberry-pineapple smoothie blended with almond milk is super easy to make. If you like to have a cold smoothie, just freeze some of the almond milk to get that extra icy texture.

**Preparation Time:** 5 Minutes

**Overall Time:** 5 Minutes

**Portions:** 1

**Produced:** 2 Cups

## Ingredients:

- 1 cup of strawberries, frozen
- 1 cup of fresh pineapple, chopped
- A further 3/4 cup of cold, unsweetened almond milk may be added.
- 1 tbsp. almond butter

## Directions:

1. Combine strawberries, pineapple, almond milk, and almond butter in a

blender.

2. Process until smooth; for a more desired consistency, simply add more almond milk.
3. Serve immediately.

**Nutritional Information:** (Per Serving)

255 Calories

11 grams of fat

39 grams of carbs

6 grams of protein

**Nutritional Profile:**

Diabetes-appropriate, bone health, dairy-free, egg-free, gluten-free, healthy aging, healthy immunity, heart-healthy, high calcium, high fiber, low sodium, low calorie, soy-free, vegan, vegetarian

**No. 5: Ham and Broccoli Breakfast Casserole**

Simply cook this wonderful broccoli casserole the night before to have it for breakfast. Reheat it in the oven in the morning, and you're ready to go!

**Preparation Time:** 20 Minutes

**Extra Time:** 8 Hours, 50 Minutes

**Overall Time:** 9 Hours, 10 Minutes

**Portions:** 8

**Produced:** 8 Servings

**Ingredients:**

- 2 cups of florets from broccoli
- Frying-pan nonstick coating
- 4 cups thawed frozen hash brown potatoes
- 2 tablespoons fresh chives, finely chopped
- 6 ounces of cooked honey ham, sliced thinly and chopped.
- 1 cup shredded, low-fat coconut Cheese, cheddar
- 8 lightly beaten eggs
- Milk without fat, 1/2 cup
- 1/2 teaspoon each of salt and black pepper
- Garlic powder, 1/4 teaspoon

**Directions:**

1. Broccoli should be cooked for three minutes in boiling, lightly salted water in a medium pot. Drain once more after rinsing with cold water.
2. Spray cooking oil in a 2-quart rectangle baking dish.
3. Toss the prepared dish with the potatoes and chives.
4. Add cheese, ham, and broccoli as garnishes.
5. Combine the eggs, milk, salt, pepper, and garlic powder in a medium bowl.
6. Over the potato mixture, pour the egg mixture.
7. Overnight chill, covered with foil.
8. Set the oven to 350 degrees Fahrenheit before serving.
9. Bake for 50 to 55 minutes, uncovered, or until eggs are done (160 degrees Fahrenheit).
10. For the final 10 minutes, if required, cover with foil to prevent over-browning.

**Nutritional Information:** (Per Serving)
219 Calories
9 grams of fat
20 grams of carbs
15 grams of protein

**Nutritional Profile:**

Diabetes-appropriate, bone health, gluten-free, healthy aging, high calcium, high protein, low calorie, nut-free, and soy-free

## No. 6: Oatmeal with Tomato and Sausage

This delicious dish adds flavor to basic oatmeal and is a filling breakfast meal made with sausage, greens, tomatoes, and herbs.

**Preparation Time:** 10 Minutes

**Extra Time:** 5 Minutes

**Overall Time:** 15 Minutes

**Portions:** 1

**Produced:** 2 1/4 Cups

**Ingredients:**

- Divide two teaspoons of canola or sunflower oil
- 1-1/2 ounces of sweet Italian chicken sausage completely cooked (1/2 link)
- 1/2 cup old-fashioned rolled oats and 1 cup low-sodium vegetable broth
- 8 grains of salt
- 1/2 cup halved grape tomatoes
- 1/3 cup of fresh herbs, such parsley or cilantro, that have been packed
- 1/2 cup baby arugula, packaged
- 1 tablespoon lightly roasted pine nuts (see tips below)
- 1-inch-long lemon wedge

**Directions:**

1. In a small nonstick or cast iron skillet, heat 1 teaspoon oil over medium heat.
2. Cook until the sausage is evenly browned, about 10 minutes.
3. Meanwhile, in a small saucepan over high heat, bring the broth to a boil.
4. Stir in the oats and salt; decrease the heat to medium; and cook, stirring periodically, for 5 minutes, or until the oats are soft and most of the liquid has been absorbed.
5. Cut the sausage into coins by slicing it thinly. Incorporate the cooked oatmeal with the sausage, tomatoes, and seasonings.
6. Transfer to a mixing bowl.
7. Drizzle with the remaining 1 tablespoon of oil and top with arugula and pine nuts.
8. If desired, garnish with a lemon wedge.

**Nutritional Information:** (Per Serving)
391 Calories
22 grams of fat
36 grams of carbs
15 grams of protein

**Nutritional Profile:**
Diabetes-appropriate, egg-free, high-protein, and soy-free.

**Tips:**

To toast pine nuts, heat them in a small, dry skillet over medium-low heat, stirring constantly, for 2 to 4 minutes, or until aromatic. Transfer to a small plate and set aside to cool.

**No. 7: Cinnamon Ginger Spiced Pear Muffins**

These diabetic-friendly muffins are ideal if you want something tasty with the ideal amount of spice.

**Preparation Time:** 20 Minutes

**Extra Time:** 40 Minutes

**Overall Time:** 1 Hour

**Portions:** 18

**Produced:** 18 Servings

**Ingredients:**

- Cooking spray that is nonstick
- 1 cup of regular flour
- 1-1/2 teaspoon baking powder 1/2 cup whole wheat flour
- 1 teaspoon of ground cinnamon
- 1/2 tablespoon baking soda
- 1/2 teaspoon ginger powder
- 1/4 teaspoon salt 1/4 teaspoon crushed nutmeg
- 1 gently beaten egg
- 1 quart of buttermilk
- 1/3 cup packed brown sugar (see tips below)
- 1/3 cup of canola oil
- 2 teaspoons of vanilla extract
- 2 medium pears
- 2 tablespoons of lemon juice
- 1 tablespoon powdered sugar

**Directions:**

1. Preheat the oven to 400 degrees Fahrenheit.
2. Cooking spray for eighteen 2-1/2 inch muffin cups.
3. Combine the next eight ingredients (through nutmeg) in a medium

43

mixing bowl.

4. In the center of the mixture, make a well.
5. Combine the next five ingredients (through vanilla) in a small bowl.
6. Stir into the flour mixture just until moistened.
7. Pears should be peeled. Brush 18 thin pear slices with lemon juice.
8. All of the remaining pear should be chopped and folded into the batter.
9. Fill the muffin cups halfway with batter.
10. Serve with pear slices on top.
11. Bake for 18 to 20 minutes, or until a toothpick inserted into the center comes out clean, swapping pan positions halfway through.
12. Remove from cups immediately and cool on wire racks.
13. Sprinkle with powdered sugar.

**Nutritional Information:** (Per Serving)

127 Calories

5 grams of fat

20 grams of carbs

2 grams of protein

**Nutritional Profile:**

Diabetes-appropriate, heart-healthy, low-calorie, low-sodium, nut-free, soy-free, vegetarian

**No. 8: Summer Skillet Vegetable and Egg Scramble**

If you notice that some of your vegetables have lost some of their prime, throw them into a skillet and scramble some eggs for a fast vegetarian breakfast meal. You can pretty much use any vegetable in this easy skillet recipe, so choose your favorites or use whatever vegetables you have on hand.

**Preparation Time:** 30 Minutes

**Overall Time:** 30 Minutes

**Portions:** 4

**Produced:** 6 Cups

**Ingredients:**

- 2 tablespoons of olive oil
- 12 ounces of finely sliced baby potatoes
- 4 cups thinly sliced veggies (14 ounces) such as mushrooms, bell peppers, and/or zucchini
- 3 thinly sliced onions, green and white sections separated
- 1 teaspoon. fresh minced herbs, such as rosemary or thyme
- 6 large eggs, lightly beaten (or 4 large eggs plus 4 egg whites)
- 2 cups packed leafy greens (2 ounces), such as baby spinach or baby kale
- 1/2 teaspoon of salt

**Directions**:

1. In a large cast-iron or nonstick skillet, heat the oil over medium heat.
2. Cover and boil, stirring occasionally, until the potatoes begin to soften, about 8 minutes.
3. Add the sliced veggies and scallions whites and simmer, uncovered, for 8 to 10 minutes, or until the vegetables are soft and lightly browned.
4. Mix in the herbs. Transfer the veggie mixture to the pan's rim.
5. Turn the heat down to medium-low.
6. In the center of the pan, place the eggs and scallion greens.
7. Cook, stirring constantly, for about 2 minutes, or until the eggs are lightly scrambled.
8. Incorporate the leafy greens into the eggs.
9. Remove from the heat and thoroughly mix. Mix in the salt.

**Nutritional Information:** (Per Serving)

254 Calories

14 grams of fat

20 grams of carbs

12 grams of protein

**Nutrition Profile:**

Diabetes-appropriate, dairy-free, gluten-free, healthy immunity, heart-healthy, high blood pressure, low added sugars, low sodium, low calorie, nut-free, soy-free, vegetarian

**No. 9: Baked Oatmeal with Pears**

This diabetic-friendly recipe has a weekend morning vibe, but you can also make it the night before and just grab and go for breakfast.

**Preparation Time:** 20 Minutes

**Extra Time:** 40 Minutes

**Overall Time:** 1 Hour

**Portions:** 6

**Produced:** 6 Servings

**Ingredients:**

- 2 cups old-fashioned oats (see tips below)
- A half cup of chopped walnuts
- 2 teaspoons of cinnamon powder
- 1 teaspoon. baking powder
- 3/4 teaspoon salt
- 1/4 teaspoon of nutmeg powder
- 1/8 teaspoon clove powder

- 2 cups almond milk (unsweetened) or 2% milk
- 1 cup plain, low-fat Greek yogurt (optional)
- 1/4 cup maple syrup
- 2 tablespoons extra-virgin olive oil
- 1 teaspoon of vanilla extract
- 2 pears, chopped tiny (approximately 2 cups; see tips below)
- 1/3 cup plain low-fat Greek yogurt (optional)

## Directions:

1. Preheat the oven to 375 degrees Fahrenheit.
2. Use cooking spray on a 9-inch square baking dish.
3. In a large mixing bowl, combine the oats, walnuts, cinnamon, baking powder, salt, nutmeg, and cloves.
4. In a medium mixing bowl, combine almond milk (or milk), 1 cup yogurt, maple syrup, oil, and vanilla extract.
5. Mix the wet and dry ingredients together. Mix in the pears gently.
6. Place the prepared baking dish on top of the mixture.
7. Bake 45 to 55 minutes, or until golden brown.
8. If preferred, top each plate with 1 tablespoon of the remaining yogurt.

## Nutritional Information: (Per Serving)

311 Calories

15 grams of fat

38 grams of carbs

9 grams of protein

## Nutritional Profile:

Diabetes-appropriate, bone health, egg-free, gluten-free, healthy aging, high calcium, low calorie, soy-free, vegetarian

## Tips:

Both ripe and unripe pears work in this recipe; however, unripe pears will hold their shape better during cooking.

Leftovers can be stored for up to 2 weeks in the freezer or up to 3 days in the refrigerator by wrapping them in parchment paper and placing them in mason jars once they have cooled.

To serve, remove the plastic wrap and microwave for 30 seconds (2 to 3 minutes if frozen). Top with 1 tablespoon Greek yogurt, if desired.

It is advised that type 2 diabetics who have celiac disease or a sensitivity to gluten use oats that are marked as "gluten-free," as oats are frequently contaminated with wheat and barley.

**No. 10: Parmesan Cloud Eggs**

Finding this really simple dish that is suitable for diabetics was a dream come true for me because I like to eat my eggs with cheese. The eggs are fluffy and light, with a generous amount of Parmesan and onions for flavor and a delicious runny yolk on top.

**Preparation Time:** 25 Minutes

**Overall Time:** 25 Minutes

**Portions:** 4

**Produced:** 4 Servings

**Ingredients:**

- 4 large eggs, separated yolks and whites
- 1 teaspoon of salt

- 1/4 cup Parmesan cheese, finely grated
- 1 finely chopped scallion
- To taste, ground pepper.

**Directions**:

1. Preheat the oven to 450 degrees Fahrenheit.
2. Using parchment paper, line a large baking sheet.
3. Coat lightly with cooking spray.
4. Separate the egg whites from the yolks, placing each yolk in a small bowl on its own.
5. In a mixing bowl, beat all of the egg whites and salt with an electric mixer on high speed until stiff.
6. With a rubber spatula, gently mix the Parmesan and scallions into the beaten whites.
7. On the prepared baking sheet, make four mounds of the egg-cheese mixture (approximately 3/4 cup each).
8. With the back of a spoon, make a well in the center of each mound.
9. Bake the egg whites for 3 minutes, or until they begin to faintly brown.
10. Take the pan out of the oven.
11. If the well has filled in during baking, recreate it using the spoon.
12. Insert a yolk into each well gently. Bake for 3 to 5 minutes more, or until the yolks are cooked but still runny.
13. Season with pepper.
14. Serve right away.

**Nutritional Information:** (Per Serving)
94 Calories
6 grams of fat
1 gram of carbs
8 grams of protein

**Nutritional Profile:**

Diabetes-appropriate, gluten-free, heart-healthy, high protein, low carbohydrate, low sodium, low calorie, nut-free, soy-free, vegetarian

## No. 11: Peanut Butter-Banana English Muffin

For those of us who can recall, the power pair of peanut butter and banana is credited to Elvis Presley, the king of rock and roll. For a delectable, healthy diabetic breakfast, simply combine banana and peanut butter, top with a toasted English muffin, and then sprinkle with a little ground cinnamon.

**Preparation Time:** 5 Minutes

**Overall Time:** 5 Minutes

**Portions:** 1

**Produced:** 1 Serving

**ingredients:**

- 1 toasted whole wheat English muffin
- 1 tablespoon of peanut butter
- 1/2 sliced banana a pinch of ground cinnamon

**Directions:**

Spread peanut butter, banana, and cinnamon on an English muffin.

**Nutritional Information:** (Per Serving)
344 Calories
10 grams of fat
57 grams of carbs
11 grams of protein

**Nutritional Profile:**

Diabetes-appropriate, dairy-free, egg-free, healthy aging, heart-healthy, high fiber, low sodium, low calorie, soy-free, vegan, vegetarian

## No. 12: Peanut Butter Banana Cinnamon Toast

More of that delicious peanut butter-banana combination that we love For a healthier option with this breakfast recipe, it is recommended to use whole wheat bread to make your toast and use natural peanut butter, which is made with just peanuts and a little salt.

As an added bonus, cinnamon has been known for many years to be one of the world's healthiest spices.

**Preparation Time:** 5 Minutes

**Overall Time:** 5 Minutes

**Portions:** 1

**Produced:** 1 Serving

**Ingredients**:

- 1 toasted piece of whole wheat bread ˙
- 1 tablespoon of peanut butter
- 1 small banana, sliced; add cinnamon to taste.

**Directions:**

Spread peanut butter on bread and top with banana slices. To taste, sprinkle with cinnamon.

**Nutritional Information:** (Per Serving)

266 Calories

9 grams of fat

38 grams of carbs

8 grams of protein

**Nutritional Profile:**

Diabetes-appropriate, dairy-free, egg-free, heart-healthy, low in added sugars, low in sodium, low in calories, soy-free, vegan, vegetarian

**No. 13: Apple Cinnamon Chia Pudding**

Your morning routine will greatly benefit from the addition of this incredibly simple chia pudding recipe. And it's made exactly like overnight oats: just mix chia with your preferred milk, let it sit overnight, then top with apples, cinnamon, and optionally, pecans for more crunch.

**Preparation Time:** 10 Minutes

**Extra Time:** 8 Hours

**Overall Time:** 8 Hours, 10 Minutes

**Portions:** 1

**Produced:** 1 Cup

**Ingredients:**

- 1/2 cup unsweetened almond milk or nondairy milk
- 2 teaspoons of chia seeds
- 2 tablespoons of pure maple syrup

- 1/4 teaspoon vanilla extract
- 1/4 teaspoon cinnamon powder
- 1/2 cup apple diced, divided
- 1 tablespoon toasted pecans, chopped

**Directions**:

1. In a small mixing bowl, combine almond milk (or other nondairy milk), chia, maple syrup, vanilla, and cinnamon.
2. Refrigerate for at least 8 hours and up to 3 days, covered.
3. Stir well before serving.
4. Pour half of the pudding, then half of the apple and pecans into a serving glass (or bowl).
5. Top with the remaining apple and pecans and the rest of the pudding.

**Nutritional Information:** (Per Serving)

233 Calories

13 grams of fat

28 grams of carbs

5 grams of protein

**Nutritional Profile:**

Diabetes-appropriate, bone health, dairy-free, egg-free, gluten-free, healthy aging, healthy pregnancy, heart-healthy, high calcium, high fiber, low sodium, low calorie, soy-free, vegan, vegetarian

**Tips:**

To remember this for later: Step 1: Refrigerate the pudding for up to 3 days. Step 2 should be completed soon before serving.

## No. 14: Peanut Butter and Chia Berry Jam English Muffin

Most of us have fond memories of eating PB&Js as children. This heart-healthy diabetic breakfast recipe includes chia seeds in the quick "jam" topping, which increases the omega-3 fatty acids.

**Cook Time:** 10 Minutes

**Overall Time:** 10 Minutes

**Portions:** 1

**Produced:** 1 Serving

**Ingredients:**

- 1/2 cup unsweetened frozen mixed berries
- 2 teaspoons of chia seeds
- 2 teaspoons of natural peanut butter
- 1 toasted whole wheat English muffin

**Directions:**

1. In a medium microwave-safe bowl, microwave the berries for 30 seconds, then toss and microwave for another 30 seconds.
2. Chia seeds should be mixed in.
3. On the English muffin, spread peanut butter.
4. Serve with the berry-chia mixture on top.

**Nutritional Information:** (Per Serving)
262 Calories
9 grams of fat
41 grams of carbs
10 grams of protein

**Nutritional Profile:**

Diabetes-appropriate, heart-healthy, low-calorie, high-fiber, dairy-free, egg-free, low sodium, high calcium, soy-free, bone health, healthy aging, vegan, vegetarian

## No. 15: Avocado Egg Toast

This super-healthy avocado egg toast will fit perfectly into your diabetic breakfast routine. You can substitute your egg for pretty much anything you want; there is no limit. I love having eggs for breakfast, and when added to the avocado toast, it makes this recipe a much healthier option. Alternatively, you can add veggies like cucumber, sprouts, or salad greens to give your avocado toast a lunch-like feel; the choice is yours.

**Cook Time:** 5 Minutes

**Overall Time:** 5 Minutes

**Portions:** 1

**Produced:** 1 Serving

**Ingredients:**

- 1/4 avocados
- 1/4 teaspoon black pepper
- 1/8 teaspoon garlic powder
- 1 toasted piece of whole wheat bread
- 1 large fried egg
- 1 teaspoon Sriracha sauce (optional)
- 1 tablespoon sliced scallions (optional)

**Directions:**

1. In a small bowl, mash the avocado with the pepper and garlic powder.
2. Place the avocado mixture and cooked egg on top of the toast.
3. If desired, garnish with Sriracha and scallions.

**Nutritional Information:** (Per Serving)
271 Calories
18 grams of fat
18 grams of carbs
12 grams of protein

**Nutritional Profile:**
Diabetes-appropriate, dairy-free, healthy aging, low added sugars, low sodium, low calorie, nut-free, soy-free, vegetarian

**Tips:**

It is advised to use multigrain or whole wheat bread because it gives your avocado toast an additional layer of flavor and fiber. Look for soft, ripe avocados when selecting them because they are ideal for mashing. more convenient to spread on toast.

**No. 16: Baby Kale Breakfast Salad with Bacon and Egg**

Having salad for breakfast may seem kind of weird, but having this healthy breakfast recipe will definitely change your mind. Kale, in itself, has been known to be a healthy option for years. And it will make sure you get your quota of healthy veggies.

**Cook Time:** 15 Minutes

**Overall Time:** 15 Minutes

**Portions:** 1

**Produced:** 1 Serving

**Ingredients:**

- 1 garlic clove, minced
- 1 tablespoon extra virgin olive oil 1 pinch of salt
- 2 teaspoons of red wine vinegar
- A pinch of black pepper
- 3 cups baby kale, lightly packed
- 1 cooked bacon slice, diced
- 1 large fried or poached egg

**Directions:**

1. To make a paste, mash garlic and salt together with the flat side of a chef's knife or a fork.
2. In a medium mixing bowl, combine the garlic paste, oil, vinegar, and pepper.
3. Toss in the kale to coat.
4. Serve the kale salad with bacon and eggs on top. Done, now eat!

**Nutritional Information:** (Per Serving)
262 Calories
22 grams of fat
6 grams of carbs
11 grams of protein

**Nutritional Profile:**
Diabetes-appropriate, dairy-free, gluten-free, healthy immunity, heart-healthy, low added sugars, low carbohydrate, low sodium, low calorie, nut-free, and soy-free

**No. 17: Morning Glory Muffins**

This popular bakery item contains everything you might want for a nutritious breakfast snack. With raisins, an apple, nuts, and toasted wheat germ on top. If you don't like raisins, you can use an equivalent amount of any other dried fruit.

**Cook Time:** 40 Minutes

**Extra Time:** 20 Minutes

**Overall Time:** 1 Hour

**Portions:** 18

**Produced:** 18 Muffins

**Ingredients:**

- 1 cup of whole wheat flour
- 1 cup unbleached all-purpose flour
- 1 tablespoon of ground cinnamon and 3/4 cup sugar
- 1 teaspoon baking powder
- 1 teaspoon baking soda
- 1/4 teaspoon salt
- 2 cups grated carrots (4 medium)
- 1 peeled and finely chopped apple
- 1/2 cup raisin
- 1 large egg
- 2 large egg whites or four teaspoons of dry egg whites (see ingredient note below), as directed on the package
- 1/2 cup of apple butter
- 1/4 cup of canola oil
- 1 tablespoon of vanilla extract
- 2 tablespoons of finely chopped walnuts or pecans

- 2 tablespoons of toasted wheat germ

## Directions:

1. Preheat the oven to 375 degrees Fahrenheit.
2. Spray 18 muffin cups with nonstick cooking spray.
3. In a large mixing bowl, combine whole wheat flour, all-purpose flour, sugar, cinnamon, baking powder, baking soda, and salt.
4. Combine carrots, apples, and raisins in a mixing bowl.
5. In a medium mixing bowl, combine the eggs, egg whites, apple butter, oil, and vanilla extract.
6. Make a well in the dry ingredients and whisk in the wet until barely incorporated with a rubber spatula.
7. Fill the prepared muffin cups about 3/4 full with the batter.
8. In a small bowl, combine walnuts and wheat germ; sprinkle over muffin tops.
9. Bake the muffins for 15 to 25 minutes, or until the tops are golden brown and bounce back when lightly touched.
10. Allow them to cool for 5 minutes in the pans.
11. Loosen the edges of the muffins and place them on a wire rack to cool.

## Nutritional Information: (Per Serving)

162 Calories
4 grams of fat
29 grams of carbs
3 grams of protein

## Nutritional Profile:

Diabetes-appropriate, heart-healthy, low-calorie, low-sodium

## Tips:

Get a head start on your morning muffins the night before by mixing up the dry and liquid ingredients separately (refrigerate liquids). In the morning, combine the two, scoop, and bake.

Ingredient Note: For meringue tops that might not reach 160°F (the temperature at which eggs are considered "safe"), dried egg whites are a smart choice because they are pasteurized. Most grocery shops have them in the baking or natural foods sections. Follow the instructions on the packaging when assembling.

DIY Muffin Cups: Line your muffin pan with muffin liners to turn your next batch of muffins or cupcakes into the ideal grab-and-go treat. No liners? No worries. Use parchment paper cut into 5-inch squares, spray each muffin cup with cooking spray, and then use a small can or bottle to place each square into the cup, forcing the paper up the sides. (It's acceptable if some of the paper protrudes over the rim.) As instructed, fill each cup.

## No. 18: Egg in a Hole, Peppers, and Avocado Salsa

This breakfast classic gets reinvigorated with colorful bell pepper rings that stand in for bread in this healthy version of an egg in a hole dish.

**Preparation Time:** 35 Minutes

**Overall Time:** 35 Minutes

**Portions:** 4

**Produced:** 4 Servings

**Ingredients;**

- 2 colored bell peppers, your choice of color
- 1/2 cup chopped red onion 1 avocado, diced

- 1/2 cup chopped fresh cilantro (plus extra for garnish) 1 jalapeno pepper, minced
- 2 seeded and diced tomatoes
- 1 lime juice, 3/4 teaspoon salt, 2 teaspoons of olive oil, 8 large eggs, 1/4 teaspoon ground pepper, divided

## Directions:

1. Remove the tops and bottoms of the bell peppers and finely chop them.
2. Seeds and membranes should be removed and discarded.
3. Each pepper should be cut into four 1/2-inch-thick rings.
4. In a medium mixing dish, combine the diced pepper, avocado, onion, jalapeno, cilantro, tomatoes, lime juice, and 1/2 teaspoon salt.
5. In a large nonstick skillet over medium heat, heat 1 teaspoon of oil.
6. Place four bell pepper rings in a bowl, then crack one egg into the center of each ring.
7. Season with 1/8 teaspoon salt and pepper. Cook for 2 to 3 minutes, or until the whites are mostly set but the yolks are still runny.
8. Cook for 1 minute more for runny yolks and 1-1/2 to 2 minutes more for firmer yolks.
9. Repeat with the remaining pepper rings and eggs on serving plates.
10. Serve with the avocado salsa and, if preferred, garnish with extra cilantro.

## Nutritional Information: (Per Serving)
285 Calories
20 grams of fat
14 grams of carbs
15 grams of protein

## Nutritional Profile:
Diabetes-appropriate, bone health, dairy-free, gluten-free, healthy aging, healthy immunity, high fiber, high protein, low carbohydrate, low calorie, nut-free, soy-free, vegetarian

## No. 19: Two-Ingredient Banana Pancakes

With literally just eggs and a banana, you can have healthy, grain-free pancakes with no added sugar. Serve with your choice of maple syrup, yogurt, or ricotta cheese to add some protein.

**Preparation Time:** 15 Minutes

**Overall Time:** 15 Minutes

**Portions:** 2

**Produced:** 2 Servings

**Ingredients:**

- 2 large eggs
- 1 medium banana

**Directions:**

1. In a blender, puree the eggs and banana until smooth.
2. Heat a large nonstick skillet over medium heat, lightly oiled (see recommendations below).
3. Drop 4 mounds of batter into the pan, using 2 tablespoons of batter for each pancake.
4. Cook for 2 to 4 minutes, or until bubbles emerge on the surface and the edges seem dry.
5. Flip the pancakes carefully with a thin spatula and cook until browned on the bottom, 1 to 2 minutes more.
6. Place the pancakes on a platter.
7. Repeat with the remaining batter, lightly oiling the pan each time.

**Nutritional Information:** (Per Serving)

    124 Calories

    5 grams of fat

    14 grams of carbs

    7 grams of protein

**Nutritional Profile:**

    Diabetes-appropriate, heart-healthy, low-calorie, low-carbohydrate, dairy-free, gluten-free, low-sodium, nut-free, soy-free, vegetarian

**Tips:**

To lightly oil a nonstick skillet, grab a paper towel, crumple it, then dab it lightly with oil and rub it over the surface of the skillet.

**No. 20: Cinnamon Roll Overnight Oats**

In just minutes, you will have this healthy diabetic breakfast. The best part is that you will have enough on hand for the rest of the week. Top with delicious vegan oats, inspired by classic cinnamon bun flavors (I love that), your choice of fresh or frozen fruit, and your favorite nuts and seeds.

**Preparation Time:** 5 Minutes

**Extra Time:** 7 Hours, 55 Minutes

**Overall Time:** 8 Hours

**Portions:** 5

**Produced:** 5 Servings

**Ingredients:**

- 2-1/2 cups old-fashioned rolled oats (see tips below)
- 2-1/2 cups unsweetened nondairy milk (almond or coconut)
- 6 teaspoons of light brown sugar
- 1-1/2 teaspoons vanilla extract
- 1-1/4 teaspoons cinnamon powder
- 1/2 teaspoon of salt

## Directions:

1. In a large mixing bowl, combine oats, milk, brown sugar, vanilla, cinnamon, and salt.
2. Divide the mixture among five 8-ounce jars.
3. Refrigerate overnight or for up to 5 days after screwing on the lids.

## Nutritional Information: (Per Serving)

191 Calories

4 grams of fat

32 grams of carbs

6 grams of protein

## Nutritional Profile:

Diabetes-appropriate, bone health, dairy-free, egg-free, gluten-free, healthy aging, heart-healthy, high calcium, low fat, low sodium, low calorie, soy-free, vegan, vegetarian

## Tips:

Type 2 diabetics that live with celiac disease or have a sensitivity to gluten should use oats that are labeled "gluten-free," as oats are often cross-contaminated with wheat and barley.

To avoid raw oats, make sure the oats are completely submerged in the liquid before covering and refrigerating.

**No. 21: Spinach and Egg Scramble with Raspberries**

This super-quick egg scramble with whole wheat bread is one of the best breakfasts for weight loss. Simply mix a couple protein-packed eggs and superfood raspberries with filling whole-grain toast and nutrient-rich spinach. These simple ingredients will help keep you full through the morning.

**Preparation Time:** 10 Minutes

**Overall Time:** 10 Minutes

**Portions:** 1

**Produced:** 1 Serving

**Ingredients:**

- 1 teaspoon of canola oil
- 1-1/2 cups baby spinach (1-1/2 oz)
- 2 large, lightly beaten eggs
- 1 teaspoon kosher salt, 1 teaspoon minced pepper
- 1 toasted slice of whole grain bread and 1/2 cup fresh raspberries

**Directions:**

1. In a small nonstick skillet over medium-high heat, heat the oil.
2. Cook until the spinach is wilted, 1 to 2 minutes, stirring frequently.
3. Place the spinach on a platter.
4. Wipe out the pan and put it over medium heat with the eggs.
5. Cook, stirring once or twice to ensure equal cooking, for 1 to 2 minutes, or until just set.
6. Add the spinach, salt, and pepper to taste.

7. With bread and strawberries, serve the scramble.

**Nutritional Information:** (Per Serving)
296 Calories
16 grams of fat
21 grams of carbs
18 grams of protein

**Nutritional Profile:**
Diabetes-appropriate, bone health, dairy-free, healthy aging, healthy immunity, heart-healthy, low sodium, low calorie, nut-free, soy-free, vegetarian

**No. 22: Breakfast Peanut Butter and Chocolate Chip Oatmeal Cakes**

Peanut butter and chocolate are such a classic combination, providing not only flavor but a boost of plant-based protein too. In the center of each muffin is a touch of peanut butter, which is a fun way to ensure that peanut butter makes it into every bite.

**Cook Time:** 15 Minutes

**Overall Time:** 50 Minutes

**Portions:** 12

**Produced:** 12 Servings

**Ingredients:**

- 3 cups rolled oats, old-fashioned
- 1-1/2 cups nonfat milk
- 1/2 cup natural creamy peanut butter, divided into 1/4 cup unsweetened applesauce

- 2 large, lightly beaten eggs
- 3 tablespoons light brown sugar, packed
- 1 teaspoon of baking powder
- 1 teaspoon of vanilla extract
- 1/2 teaspoon of salt
- 1/4 cup semisweet, tiny chocolate chips

**Equipment:** muffin tin with 12 (1/2 cup) cups

**Directions:**

1. Preheat the oven to 375 degrees Fahrenheit.
2. Coat a 12-cup muffin pan with nonstick cooking spray.
3. In a large mixing bowl, combine oats, milk, 1/4 cup peanut butter, applesauce, eggs, brown sugar, baking powder, vanilla, and salt.
4. Fill each muffin cup halfway with batter, then evenly distribute the remaining 1/4 cup of peanut butter and chocolate chips, about 1 teaspoon each.
5. Cover with roughly 2 tablespoons of the remaining batter.
6. Bake for 25 minutes, or until a toothpick inserted into the center comes out clean.
7. Allow to cool in the pan for 10 minutes before turning out onto a wire rack.
8. Warm or at room temperature, serve.

**Nutritional Information:** (Per Serving)
204 Calories
9 grams of fat
24 grams of carbs
7 grams of protein

**Nutritional Profile:**
Diabetes-appropriate, gluten-free, heart-healthy, high fiber, high protein,

low sodium, soy-free, vegetarian

**Tips:**

To remember this for later: Oatmeal cakes can be frozen in an airtight container for up to 3 months.

Microwave 1 oatmeal cake in 30-second increments until heated thoroughly. Alternatively, store oatmeal cakes in an airtight container in the refrigerator for up to 2 days.

## No. 23: Apple, Bacon, and Sweet Potato Mini Casseroles

In literally just an hour, you will love having these sweet and savory mini casseroles. Refrigerate or freeze the leftovers to enjoy later.

**Preparation Time:** 30 Minutes

**Extra Time:** 30 Minutes

**Overall Time:** 1 Hour

**Portions:** 6

**Produced:** 6 Servings

**Ingredients:**

- Cooking spray that is nonstick
- 10 slices of low-sodium, lower-fat bacon
- 2 cups cooked apples, chopped
- 1/2 cup finely chopped onion
- 1 sweet potato, peeled and sliced into 1/4-inch chunks, 10 oz.

- 2 teaspoons fresh thyme plucked or 1/2 teaspoon dried thyme, crushed, 1/4 teaspoon black pepper
- 1/2 cup thawed refrigerated or frozen egg product or 6 lightly beaten eggs
- 3/4 cup nonfat milk
- 3 ounces shredded reduced-fat cheddar cheese

## Directions:

1. Preheat the oven to 350 degrees Fahrenheit.
2. Spray twelve 2-1/2-inch muffin cups with cooking spray.
3. Four of the bacon pieces should be cut crosswise into thirds; the remaining bacon should be chopped.
4. Cook big bacon chunks in a 12-inch pan over medium heat until crisp.
5. Discard the drippings after draining the bacon on paper towels.
6. To the skillet, add the diced bacon, apples, and onion.
7. Cook for 5 minutes, stirring occasionally, over medium heat.
8. Cook for 10 minutes, or until the sweet potato is cooked, stirring periodically.
9. Mix in the thyme and pepper.
10. Divide the potato mixture evenly among the muffin cups.
11. Combine the egg and milk in a medium bowl; pour over the potato mixture (cups will be filled).
12. Serve with cheese on top.
13. Bake for 25 minutes, or until puffy and a knife inserted into the center comes out clean.
14. Cool for 5 minutes in the cups. Take them out of the cups.
15. Large bacon slices should be placed on top. Serve hot.

## Nutritional Information: (Per Serving)
198 Calories
6 grams of fat
22 grams of carbs

15 grams of protein

**Nutritional Profile:**
Diabetes-appropriate, gluten-free, heart-healthy, low-sodium, low-calorie, nut-free, and soy-free

**No. 24: Breakfast Tostada**

For those of us who love having a bit of a Latin flavor for breakfast. This super simple Mexican-inspired breakfast recipe brings tons of flavor to your plate, all in just 20 minutes.

**Cook Time:** 20 Minutes

**Overall Time:** 20 Minutes

**Portions**

**Produced:** 1 Serving

**Ingredients:**

- 1/4 cup drained black beans with no additional sodium
- 2 tablespoons of water
- 1/4 teaspoon taco seasoning, divided into two tablespoons of lime juice
- 1/4 avocado (mashed)
- 1/4 cup Roma tomato, diced
- 1 tablespoon white onion, chopped
- 1 whole wheat or corn tortilla (6 inches)
- Cooking spray that is nonstick
- 1 large egg
- 1/4 cup romaine lettuce, shredded

## Directions:

1. In a microwave-safe bowl, combine black beans, water, 1 tablespoon lime juice, and taco seasoning.
2. Microwave for 2 minutes on high.
3. Mash the beans into a pulp with a fork; set aside.
4. In a small bowl, mash the avocado with a fork.
5. Combine the tomato, onion, remaining 1 tablespoon lime juice, and a pinch of salt in a mixing bowl. Place aside.
6. Coat both sides of the tortilla with frying spray. Melt butter in a small nonstick skillet over medium heat.
7. Toast the tortilla, flipping once, until crisp and lightly browned on both sides, 3 to 4 minutes. Place on a platter.
8. Reduce the heat to medium-low after cracking the egg into the pan.
9. Cook, flipping once if preferred, for 2 to 3 minutes, or until the white is set.
10. Layer the bean mixture, avocado mixture, and lettuce on the tortilla to make the tostada.

Finish with the egg.

## Nutritional Information: (Per Serving)
365 Calories
19 grams of fat
40 grams of carbs
15 grams of protein

## Nutritional Profile:
Diabetes-appropriate, dairy-free, healthy pregnancy, high protein, nut-free, soy-free, vegetarian

## No. 25: Egg Sandwiches with Rosemary, Tomato, and Feta

I really enjoy eating these, and knowing that these hearty breakfast sandwiches are packed with ingredients popular in the Mediterranean diet, including feta, tomato, and spinach, makes me want to have them over and over. Enjoy!

**Preparation Time:** 5 Minutes

**Extra Time:** 15 Minutes

**Overall Time:** 20 Minutes

**Portions:** 4

**Produced:** 4 Servings

**Ingredients:**

- 4 sandwich thins, multigrain
- 4 teaspoons of olive oil
- 1/2 teaspoon crushed dry rosemary or 1 tablespoon chopped fresh rosemary
- 4 eggs
- 2 cups baby spinach leaves, fresh
- 8 thin slices of a medium tomato
- 4 tablespoons of low-fat feta cheese
- 1/8 teaspoon kosher salt
- Ground black pepper, freshly ground

**Equipment:** rimmed baking sheet

**Directions:**

1. Preheat the oven to 375 degrees Fahrenheit.

2. Thinly slice the sandwich and brush the sliced sides with 2 tablespoons of olive oil.
3. Place on a rimmed baking sheet and toast for 5 minutes, or until the edges are light golden and crisp.
4. Meanwhile, heat the remaining 2 tablespoons of olive oil and rosemary in a large skillet over medium-high heat.
5. Break the eggs into a skillet, one at a time. Cook for 1 minute, or until the whites are set but the yolks are runny.
6. Using a spatula, break the yolks. Cook until the eggs are done on the other side.
7. Take the pan off the heat.
8. Place the toasted sandwich's thin bottom halves on four serving dishes.
9. Place spinach between sandwich slices on plates.
10. 2 tomato slices, an egg, and 1 tablespoon feta cheese on top of each; season with salt and pepper to taste.
11. Top with the remaining thin sandwich halves.

**Nutritional Information:** (Per Serving)
242 Calories
12 grams of fat
25 grams of carbs
13 grams of protein

**Nutritional Profile:**
Diabetes-appropriate, healthy aging, healthy immunity, heart-healthy, low sodium, low calorie, nut-free, vegetarian

**No. 26: Quick-Cooking Oats**

Sometimes quicker is better, and at breakfast, that can certainly be the case. This super easy oatmeal recipe teaches you the best basic methods so you get creamy, tender oats every time. Top it with your favorite flavors of your choice.

**Preparation Time:** 5 Minutes

**Overall Time:** 5 Minutes

**Portions:** 1

**Produced:** 1 Cup

**Ingredients:**

- 1 cup of water or skim milk
- 1 teaspoon of salt
- 1/2 cup quick-cooking oats (see tips below)
- 1 ounce of low-fat milk, per serving
- 1 to 2 teaspoons of honey, cane sugar, or brown sugar, per serving
- 1 teaspoon of cinnamon

**Directions:**

1. In a small saucepan, combine water (or milk) and salt. Bring the water to a boil.
2. Reduce heat to medium and stir in the oats for 1 minute.
3. Remove from the heat, cover, and let stand for 2-3 minutes.
4. In a 2-cup microwave-safe bowl, combine the water (or milk), salt, and oats.
5. Microwave for 1-1/2 to 2 minutes on high. Before serving, give it a good stir.
6. Toppings such as milk, sweetener, cinnamon, dried fruits, and nuts are optional.

**Nutritional Information:** (Per Serving)
150 Calories
3 grams of fat

27 grams of carbs

5 grams of protein

**Nutritional Profile:**

Diabetes-appropriate, dairy-free, egg-free, gluten-free, heart-healthy, low-fat, low-sodium, low-calorie, nut-free, soy-free, vegan, vegetarian

**Tips:**

If your recipe calls for quick oats but you only have rolled oats, toss them in a food processor and pulse for a few seconds to break them down into tiny bits. If you have quick oats and a recipe that asks for rolled oats, you can substitute quick oats.

Quick oats and rolled oats can both be used in baking and cooking; however, their texture may be less pronounced in baked items, and rolled oats may need to be cooked for longer than the time specified in the recipe for stovetop cooking.

Type 2 diabetics who have celiac disease or a gluten sensitivity should consume oats labeled "gluten-free," as oats are frequently cross-contaminated with wheat and barley.

### No. 27: Breakfast Strawberry & Cream Cheese Oatmeal Cakes

I enjoy having fresh strawberries, and when I include them with this recipe, it adds that perfect touch of natural sweetness to these breakfast oatmeal cakes. When strawberries are not in season, you can easily substitute frozen ones.

**Cook Time:** 15 Minutes

**Overall Time:** 50 Minutes

**Portions:** 12

**Produced:** 12 Servings

**Ingredients:**

- 1/4 cup room-temperature reduced-fat cream cheese
- 1 tablespoon of strawberry jam
- 3 cups rolled oats, old-fashioned
- 1/4 cup nonfat milk
- 1/3 cup brown sugar, packed
- 1/4 cup applesauce, unsweetened
- 2 large, lightly beaten eggs
- 1 teaspoon of baking powder
- 1 teaspoon of vanilla extract
- 1/2 teaspoon of salt
- 1/4 cup chopped fresh or frozen strawberries

**Equipment:** muffin tin with 12 (1/2 cup) cups

**Directions:**

1. Preheat the oven to 375 degrees Fahrenheit.
2. Coat a 12-cup muffin pan with nonstick cooking spray.
3. In a small mixing dish, combine the cream cheese and jam.
4. In a large mixing bowl, combine oats, milk, brown sugar, applesauce, eggs, baking powder, vanilla, and salt.
5. 1/2 cup of strawberries should be folded in.
6. Fill 2 to 3 tablespoons of batter into each prepared muffin cup, then top with a dollop of strawberry cream cheese and some of the remaining 1/4 cup of strawberries.
7. Cover with the remaining batter and gently press to compact.
8. Bake for 25 to 30 minutes, or until a toothpick inserted into the center

comes out clean.

9. Allow it to cool for 10 minutes in the pan.

10. To release the oatmeal cakes, run a knife down the edges of the muffin cups, then turn them out onto a wire rack.

11. Warm or at room temperature, serve.

**Nutritional Information:** (Per Serving)

137 Calories

3 grams of fat

24 grams of carbs

5 grams of protein

**Nutritional Profile:**

Diabetes-appropriate, gluten-free, heart-healthy, nut-free, soy-free, vegetarian

**Tips:**

Freeze oatmeal cakes in an airtight jar for up to 3 months to keep them for later. Microwave 1 oatmeal cake in 30-second increments until heated thoroughly. You can also store your oatmeal cakes in an airtight jar in the refrigerator for up to 2 days.

**No. 28: Bacon and Egg Breakfast Wraps**

I love having breakfast wraps. So making these super easy Mexican-inspired bacon and egg breakfast wraps rolled in a tortilla is an absolute dream!

**Preparation Time:** 25 Minutes

**Overall Time:** 25 Minutes

**Portions:** 4

**Produced:** 4 Servings

**Ingredients:**

- 4 bacon pieces, chopped
- 1 cup fresh mushrooms, chopped
- 1/4 teaspoon chili powder 1/2 cup minced green sweet pepper (1 small)
- 1/4 teaspoon black pepper, ground
- 1/8 teaspoon salt
- 1/4 cup chopped seeded tomato 1 cup refrigerated or frozen egg product, thawed
- A few drops of hot pepper sauce, bottled
- Four (8-inch) warmed flour tortillas (see tips below)

**Directions:**

1. Cook bacon in a large nonstick skillet over medium heat until crisp.
2. Remove the bacon from the skillet with a slotted spoon, saving 1 tablespoon of the drippings in the skillet (discard the other drippings).
3. Using paper towels, drain the bacon.
4. To the saved drippings in the skillet, add the mushrooms, sweet pepper, chili powder, pepper, and salt; simmer and stir for about 3 minutes, or until the vegetables are soft.
5. Pour the egg mixture into the skillet with the vegetables.
6. Lift and fold the egg mixture with a spatula or a large spoon so that the uncooked portion flows underneath.
7. Cook for another 2 minutes over medium heat, or until the egg is cooked through but still glossy and wet.
8. Incorporate the cooked bacon, tomatoes, and spicy pepper sauce.
9. Divide the egg mixture among the tortillas, roll them up, and serve right away.

**Nutritional Information:** (Per Serving)

195 Calories

9 grams of fat

18 grams of carbs

11 grams of protein

**Nutritional Profile:**

Diabetes-appropriate, dairy-free, heart-healthy, low sodium, low calorie, nut-free, and soy-free

**Tips:**

To warm your tortillas, preheat the oven to 350°F. Make sure to tightly cover your tortillas with foil. Bake for 10 minutes or until thoroughly heated.

**No. 29: Berry Banana Cauliflower Smoothie**

When you need to sneak in your veggie quota for the morning. Simply make this breakfast smoothie that has added thickness and creaminess and has a subtly sweet cauliflower flavor that features the fruity flavors of bananas and berries.

**Preparation Time:** 5 Minutes

**Extra Time:** 5 Minutes

**Overall Time:** 10 Minutes

**Portions:** 2

**Produced:** 2 Smoothies

**Ingredients:**

- 1 cup of riced cauliflower, frozen
- 1/2 cup mixed frozen berries
- 1 cup frozen, sliced banana
- 2 cups plain, unsweetened almond milk
- 2 teaspoons of maple syrup

**Directions:**

1. In a blender, combine the cauliflower, berries, banana, almond milk, and maple syrup.
2. Blend for 3–4 minutes, or until smooth.

**Nutritional Information:** (Per Serving)

149 Calories

3 grams of fat

29 grams of carbs

3 grams of protein

**Nutritional Profile:**

Diabetes-appropriate, heart-healthy, low-calorie, low-fat, dairy-free, egg-free, gluten-free, low sodium, high calcium, soy-free, bone health, healthy aging, healthy immunity, vegan, vegetarian

**No. 30: Steel-Cut Oatmeal**

This classic version became a part of my morning breakfast ritual after I discovered how to make it. And why not? It's nutritious, chewy, and will keep you satisfied until lunch.

**Preparation Time:** 30 Minutes

**Overall Time:** 30 Minutes

**Portions:** 1

**Produced:** 1 Cup

**Ingredients:**

- 1 cup of water or skim milk
- 1/4 cup steel-cut oats (see tips below)
- 1 ounce of low-fat milk per serving
- 1 teaspoon or 2 teaspoons of honey, cane sugar, or brown sugar
- 1 teaspoon of cinnamon

**Directions:**

1. In a small saucepan, combine water (or milk) and salt. Bring the water to a boil.
2. Reduce heat to low and mix in oats; simmer, stirring regularly, until oats are the desired texture, 20 to 30 minutes.
3. Toppings such as milk, sweetener, cinnamon, dried fruits, or nuts are optional.

**Nutritional Information:** (Per Serving)
150 Calories
3 grams of fat
27 grams of carbs
5 grams of protein

**Nutritional Profile:**
Diabetes-appropriate, dairy-free, gluten-free, heart-healthy, low-fat, low-sodium, low-calorie, nut-free, soy-free, vegan, vegetarian

**Tips:**

Type 2 diabetics who have celiac disease or a gluten sensitivity should consume oats labeled "gluten-free," as oats are frequently cross-contaminated with wheat and barley.

**In Summary:**

This is far from a comprehensive list of type 2 diabetes breakfast recipes. I've experimented with these recipes many times over the years, mixing and matching, and I encourage you to do the same. Make these breakfast recipes to fit your specific needs.

In addition, I recommend that you use these breakfast recipes to plan your meals with the planners that I have included. Enjoy!

# 7

# Lunch Recipes

For most of us, we lead a very busy life. Finding a fast, easy lunch for a type 2 diabetic is somewhat of a challenge; most of the time, we don't have time to think about what we eat for lunch. With that, I have compiled a list of some of my favorite lunch recipes in full detail. They are super healthy and easy enough to make to last you for the week.

With complex carbs like whole grains and legumes, low amounts of saturated fat, and low sodium counts within our recipe parameters, these lunch recipes are perfect for type 2 diabetics and go really well with the meal planners I have included.

**No. 1: Vegan Bistro Lunch Box**

This one gets a lot of use because it's ideal for a picnic or packing a business lunch. This vegan bistro box includes crunchy veggies inspired by the Mediterranean diet, pita bread, creamy hummus, and olives. It just took 5 minutes!

**Preparation Time:** 5 Minutes

**Total Time:** 5 Minutes

**Portions:** 1

**Produced:** 1 Box

**Ingredients:**

- 1/4 cup hummus
- 1/2 whole wheat pita bread, divided into 4 wedges
- 2 tablespoons olives (mixed)
- 1 Persian cucumber or 1/2 English cucumber spear 1/4 large sliced red bell pepper 1/4 teaspoon chopped fresh dill

**Directions:**

1. Fill a 4-cup divided, sealed container halfway with hummus, pita, olives, cucumber, and bell peppers.
2. If desired, separate the hummus and olives by placing them in silicone baking cups before arranging.
3. Dill should be sprinkled over the cucumber.
4. Store in the refrigerator until ready to use.

**Nutritional Information** (per serving)

194 Calories

9 grams of fat

23 grams of carbs

8 grams of protein

**Nutritional Profile:**

Diabetes-appropriate, heart-healthy, low-calorie, diary-free, egg-free, low-sodium, nut-free, soy-free, vegan, vegetarian

**Tips:**

Refrigerate for up to 1 day if you want to keep it for later.

## No. 2: Meal-Prep Curried Chicken Bowls

If you wish to keep it, refrigerate it for up to one day. Curry is one of my favorite spices, and this easy recipe takes no time to prepare. You can make these quick meal prep bowls in just a few minutes with a sheet pan and some cooked, healthy grains to be used afterwards. You can also keep them in the fridge for a fast weeknight meal or a nutritious grab-and-go lunch during the week.

**Preparation Time:** 5 Minutes

**Total Time:** 5 Minutes

**Portions:** 4

**Produced:** 4 Servings

**Ingredients:**

- 1 cup brown rice, cooked
- 1 cup quinoa, cooked
- 1/4 cup chopped fresh cilantro 1 pound of cooked curried chicken
- 1/4 cup scallions, thinly sliced

**Directions:**

1. Combine rice and quinoa in a mixing bowl; divide into four single-serving containers with lids.
2. Distribute the chicken, cilantro, and scallions evenly.
3. Refrigerate for up to 4 days after sealing the containers.

**Nutritional Information** (per serving)

274 Calories

7 grams of fat

28 grams of carbs

24 grams of protein

**Nutritional Profile:**

Diabetes-appropriate, egg-free, gluten-free, heart-healthy, high protein, low sodium, low calorie, nut-free, and soy-free

**Tips:**

Refrigerate containers for up to 4 days if you want to store them for later.

**No. 3: Avocado, Tomato, and Chicken Sandwich**

This healthy chicken sandwich recipe is perfect for those quick lunch breaks. The avocado is mashed to create a healthy, creamy spread.

**Cook Time:** 5 Minutes

**Total Time:** 5 Minutes

**Portions:** 1

**Produced:** 1 Serving, sandwich each

**Ingredients:**

- 1/4 ripe avocado 1/4 piece of multigrain bread
- 3 ounces of cooked boneless, skinless chicken breast (see tips below)
- 2 tomato slices

## Directions:

1. Toast the bread. With a fork, mash the avocado and spread it on one slice of toast.
2. Top with the remaining toast, chicken, and tomato.

## Nutritional Information (per serving)
347 Calories
12 grams of fat
28 grams of carbs
31 grams of protein

## Nutritional Profile:
Diabetes-appropriate, heart-healthy, low-calorie, high-fiber, dairy-free, low-sodium, healthy aging, low added sugars

## Tips:

If you don't have cooked chicken, you can poach it to use in a recipe. Place boneless, skinless chicken breasts in a skillet or saucepan. Add lightly salted water to cover and bring to a boil.

Cover, reduce heat to a simmer, and cook until no longer pink in the middle, 10 to 15 minutes, depending on size. 8 ounces of raw, boneless, skinless chicken breast yields about 1 cup of sliced, diced, or shredded cooked chicken.

## No. 4: 10-Minute Tuna Melt

This classic sandwich uses mayonnaise, but don't worry, it is used in a much different area than it usually is. The mayonnaise is brushed on the outside of the sandwich in place of butter to make the sandwich golden and crispy as it heats in a skillet. Plain Greek yogurt takes mayo's place in the salad along with crunchy celery, roasted red bell peppers, and scallions for a satisfying lunch with less saturated fat.

**Cook Time:** 10 Minutes

**Total Time:** 10 Minutes

**Portions:** 2

**Produced:** 2 Servings

**Ingredients:**

- One 5 oz. water-packed tuna, no salt added, drained
- 1 sliced, tiny celery stalk
- 2 tablespoons chopped roasted red pepper from a jar
- 1 minced scallion
- 3 tablespoons plain, low-fat Greek yogurt
- 1/4 teaspoon powdered pepper 1 teaspoon Dijon mustard
- 4 teaspoons mayonnaise (or softened butter)
- 4 slices of whole wheat bread
- 2 oz. sharp cheddar cheese

**Directions:**

1. In a medium mixing bowl, combine tuna, celery, roasted red pepper, scallions, yogurt, mustard, and pepper.
2. On one side of each slice of bread, spread 1 teaspoon mayonnaise (or butter).
3. Top each with half of the tuna mixture, 1 slice of cheese, and another slice of bread, mayonnaise side up.
4. Melt butter in a large skillet over medium heat.
5. Place the sandwiches in the pan and cook, flipping once, for 3 to 5 minutes per side, or until the cheese is melted and the bread is brown.

6. Serve right away.

**Nutritional Information** (per serving)

382 Calories

13 grams of fat

29 grams of carbs

34 grams of protein

**Nutritional Profile:**

Diabetes-appropriate, high-protein, nut-free

**No. 5: Egg Salad English Muffin Sandwich**

This quick lunch recipe sandwich tastes amazing, and when you boil eggs ahead of time, it makes this sandwich that much easier to create, and you can enjoy a delightful lunchtime egg salad. When adding the flavorful leafy carrot tops to the sandwich, it is like getting herbs for free!

**Cook Time:** 10 Minutes

**Total Time:** 10 Minutes

**Portions:** 1

**Produced:** 1 Serving

**Ingredients:**

- 1 split whole wheat English muffin
- 1 tablespoon of olive oil
- 2 medium carrots with tops (see tips below)
- 2 large hard-boiled eggs (see below for instructions)
- 1 tablespoon mayonnaise plus 1 teaspoon

- 1 large shredded romaine lettuce leaf

**Directions:**

1. Preheat a grill pan or nonstick skillet over medium-high heat.
2. Oil the cut sides of the English muffin halves.
3. 1 to 2 minutes per side, grill the muffins until both sides are lightly browned.
4. If preferred, peel the carrots and chop them into sticks. Chop 1 tablespoon of the carrot tops.
5. Place the hard-boiled eggs in a small bowl and dice them.
6. Stir in the mayonnaise and carrot tops until well mixed.
7. Top with the egg salad and divide the lettuce between the grilled muffin pieces.
8. Carrots should be served on the side.

**Nutritional Information** (per serving)
497 Calories
30 grams of fat
37 grams of carbs
20 grams of protein

**Nutritional Profile:**
Diabetes-appropriate

**Tips:**

If you can't find carrots with tops, use 1/2 teaspoon dried dill or 1 minced fresh scallion in place of the carrot leaves in Step 2.

To reduce saturated fat, use a combination of 1 large hard-boiled egg and the whites from 2 large hard-boiled eggs. Reserve the cooked egg yolks for another purpose, such as topping a green salad.

## No. 6: Pulled Chicken and Pickled Veggie Wraps

Lunch is a treat when you have these colorful chicken wraps. Marinated radishes, onions, and carrots add a salty crunch and a healthy serving of vegetables!

**Preparation Time:** 30 Minutes

**Extra Time:** 1 Hour

**Total Time:** 1 Hour, 30 Minutes

**Portions:** 8

**Produced:** 8 Servings

**Ingredients:**

- 2 cups carrots, julienned or roughly shredded
- 1 cup radishes, julienne
- 1 cup red onion, thinly sliced
- 1/2 cup white vinegar
- 2 tablespoons of sugar
- 1 tablespoon of salt
- 1/2 cup mayonnaise (light)
- 1 teaspoon Sriracha, add more to taste
- 8 low-carb whole wheat tortillas (7 to 8 inches), such as La Tortilla Factory
- 8 leaves of Bibb and/or red leaf lettuce
- 2-2/3 cups cooked shredded chicken breast

**Directions:**

1. In a tight plastic bag, combine carrots, radishes, onion, vinegar, sugar,

and salt.

2. Coat the other side.

3. Place the bag in a shallow dish and place it in the refrigerator for 1 hour to marinate.

4. In a small mixing dish, combine mayonnaise and Sriracha.

5. Remove the pickled veggies from the marinade and set aside.

6. 1 tablespoon of the mayonnaise mixture should be spread on each tortilla.

7. Roll up the lettuce, chicken, and pickled vegetables.

8. Wrap with plastic wrap and place in the refrigerator for up to 24 hours.

9. If desired, drizzle with additional Sriracha.

## Nutritional Information (per serving)

248 Calories

10 grams of fat

27 grams of carbs

23 grams of protein

## Nutritional Profile:

Diabetes-appropriate, low-calorie, high-fiber, dairy-free, nut-free, and healthy aging

## Tips:

Sugar substitute: It is not recommended to use a sugar substitute for this recipe.

## No. 7: Chicken Avocado BLT Wrap

Who doesn't love a BLT? In this Mexican-inspired version, this super-easy recipe has chicken and avocado all wrapped in a tortilla, making it easy to eat.

**Preparation Time:** 10 Minutes

**Total Time:** 10 Minutes

**Portions:** 1

**Produced:** 1 Serving

**Ingredients:**

- 1 cup guacamole (100 calories)
- One 8-inch whole wheat low-carb tortilla
- 2/3 cup fresh baby spinach leaves
- 2 ounces shredded cooked chicken breast (1/2 cup)
- 4 halved cherry tomatoes
- 1 cooked and drained slice of lower sodium, lower fat bacon
- 1/2 cup raisins

**Directions:**

1. Guacamole should be spread on the tortilla.
2. Serve with spinach, chicken, tomatoes, and bacon on top.
3. Roll up.
4. Serve with fresh grapes.

**Nutritional Information** (per serving)
340 Calories
15 grams of fat
33 grams of carbs
28 grams of protein

**Nutritional Profile:**
Diabetes-appropriate, dairy-free, egg-free, healthy aging, healthy immunity, heart-healthy, high fiber, high protein, low sodium, low calorie, and nut-free

## No. 8: Curried Chicken Apple Wraps

At first glance, these ingredients might seem a bit weird, but shredded chicken and chopped green apples are a wonderful combination in this fast and easy curried sandwich wrap.

**Preparation Time:** 20 Minutes

**Total Time:** 20 Minutes

**Portions:** 2

**Produced:** 2 Servings

**Ingredients:**

- 1 cup cooked, shredded chicken breast
- 1/2 cup green apple, chopped
- 2 tablespoons chopped red onion
- 2 teaspoons light mayonnaise
- 2 tbsp fat-free plain Greek yogurt
- 1/4 teaspoon curry powder
- 2 warmed 6- to 7-inch low-carb flour tortillas (such as La Tortilla Factory® brand)
- 12 baby spinach leaves or 2 leaves lettuce

**Directions:**

1. In a small mixing dish, combine the chicken, apple, onion, mayonnaise, yogurt, and curry powder.
2. Wrap the tortillas in spinach (or lettuce).
3. Roll up the tortillas and top them with the chicken salad.
4. Toothpicks can be used to fasten them if desired.

**Nutritional Information** (per serving)

  244 Calories

  10 grams of fat

  17 grams of carbs

  28 grams of protein

**Nutritional Profile:**

  Diabetes-appropriate, healthy aging, heart-healthy, high fiber, high protein, low sodium, low calorie, nut-free

**Tips:**

Preheat the oven to 350°F to warm the tortillas. Wrap the tortillas tightly in foil. Bake for 10 minutes or until thoroughly heated.

**No. 9: Ham & Cheese Sandwich Wrap**

Instead of a boring old ham and cheese sandwich for lunch, try this wrap! The broccoli sprouts offer crispness and nutrition, while the honey mustard sweetens the dish.

**Preparation Time:** 5 Minutes

**Total Time:** 5 Minutes

**Portions:** 1

**Produced:** 1 Serving

**Ingredients:**

- 1 whole wheat tortilla with high fiber and low carbs
- 1 tablespoon honey mustard

- 1 slice of lunch meat (low-sodium ham)
- 3 tablespoons shredded reduced-fat cheddar cheese
- 1/2 cup tomato, diced
- 1 cup sprouted broccoli
- 1 cup sugar snap peas, raw

**Directions:**

1. On the tortilla, spread mustard.
2. On top, layer ham, cheddar cheese, tomatoes, and broccoli sprouts.
3. Make a wrap out of it.
4. Serve alongside snap peas.

**Nutritional Information** (per serving)

234 Calories

7 grams of fat

28 grams of carbs

20 grams of protein

**Nutritional Profile:**

Diabetes-appropriate, heart-healthy, low-calorie, high-fiber, egg-free, low-sodium, nut-free, healthy aging

**No. 10: Strawberry and Cream Cheese Sandwich**

This is a delightful and mouthwatering dish made with sliced strawberries and reduced-fat cream cheese that comes together in a sandwich for a quick and healthy lunchbox treat.

**Cook Time:** 5 Minutes

**Total Time:** 5 Minutes

**Portions:** 1

**Produced:** 1 Serving

**Ingredients:**

- 1 cup reduced-fat cream cheese
- 1/4 teaspoon of honey
- 2 slices of extremely thin whole wheat sandwich bread
- 1/8 teaspoon freshly grated orange zest
- 2 medium-sized sliced strawberries

**Directions:**

1. In a mixing dish, combine cream cheese, honey, and orange zest.
2. Spread the cheese mixture on the bread.
3. Layer cut strawberries on one piece of bread, then the other.

**Nutritional Information** (per serving)

123 Calories

4 grams of fat

19 grams of carbs

4 grams of protein

**Nutritional Profile:**

Diabetes-appropriate, heart-healthy, low in added sugars, low in sodium, low in calories, vegetarian

## No. 11: Hawaiian Steak Fajitas with Grilled Pineapple Salsa

In this wonderful dish, it's all about the prep: peel pineapple, preslice peppers and onions, and make fresh pico de gallo. This quick, healthy recipe comes together in a hurry. If you like, you can substitute chicken tenders for the steak. Make some margaritas and throw a party. What more could you want?

**Cook Time:** 30 Minutes

**Total Time:** 30 Minutes

**Portions:** 4

**Produced:** 4 Servings

**Ingredients:**

- 1 pound of trimmed strip steak
- 4 cups (approximately 12 ounces) of pre-sliced fresh pepper and onion mix
- 2 tablespoons extra-virgin olive oil
- 1/4 teaspoon salt, 1/4 teaspoon pepper
- 2 ounces of fresh pineapple, peeled (3/4 inch thick; approximately 4 ounces)
- 3 tablespoons teriyaki sauce (reduced sodium)
- 1/4 cup pico de gallo or another type of fresh tomato salsa
- 8 warmed corn tortillas

**Directions:**

1. Preheat the grill to high and place a grill basket on one half of it.
2. Cut the meat into 1/4-inch-thick pieces crosswise.
3. In a medium mixing dish, combine the peppers and onions, oil, salt, and pepper.
4. Grill the steak and veggies in the grill basket for 8 to 10 minutes, stirring once or twice, until the vegetables are tender and charred.
5. Grill the pineapple, rotating once, until slightly browned, about 2 minutes per side, on the other side of the grill rack.

6. Toss the meat and vegetables with the teriyaki sauce in a large mixing bowl.
7. Dice the pineapple and blend it with the pico de gallo (or salsa) in a small bowl.
8. Serve the steak and vegetables with the salsa on tortillas.

**Nutritional Information** (per serving)

378 Calories

14 grams of fat

37 grams of carbs

27 grams of protein

**Nutritional Profile:**

Diabetes-appropriate, dairy-free, egg-free, gluten-free, healthy aging, healthy immunity, heart-healthy, high protein, low added sugars, low sodium, low calorie, nut-free, and soy-free

**No. 12: A Classic Hamburger for Two**

I understand that eating hamburgers for a type 2 diabetic may not seem like a good choice, but it's the ingredients in the burger that make it a healthy alternative for type 2 diabetics. It is a pretty simple meal that is also a healthy option. When the onions are slowly cooked, they provide moisture and flavor to these lean beef burgers for two. A quick blend of mayonnaise, ketchup, relish, and vinegar makes the perfect tangy, sweet, and creamy "special sauce" for this burger. I love the dill relish here, but you can use sweet relish if you prefer it. Serve with sweet potato fries.

**Cook Time:** 45 Minutes

**Total Time:** 45 Minutes

**Portions:** 2

**Produced:** 2 Servings

**Ingredients:**

- 1 sliced, tiny onion
- 1-1/2 tablespoons of canola oil
- 3 tablespoons ketchup, split
- 1 tablespoon mayonnaise (low-fat)
- 1 teaspoon pickled dill relish
- 1/2 teaspoon white vinegar, distilled
- 8 ounces ground beef, lean
- 1 teaspoon Worcestershire or steak sauce
- 1/4 teaspoon freshly ground pepper
- 2 toasted sesame seed or other hamburger buns
- 2 tomato slices
- 2 green leaf lettuce leaves

**Directions:**

1. Preheat the grill to medium-high heat (or use the stove top variation).
2. In a small skillet, combine the onion, oil, and 1-1/2 teaspoons ketchup.
3. Cook, covered, over medium-high heat for 4 to 6 minutes, or until the onion is softened.
4. Reduce the heat to medium low, cover, and simmer until the potatoes are very soft, 5 to 8 minutes more.
5. Allow it to cool for a few minutes in a medium bowl.
6. Meanwhile, in a separate bowl, combine the remaining 1-1/2 teaspoons of ketchup, mayonnaise, relish, and vinegar. Place aside.
7. To the onion, add the beef, Worcestershire (or steak sauce), and pepper and gently blend without over mixing. Form into two 3/4-inch-thick patties.
8. Oil the grill rack (see tips below). Grill the burgers for 4 to 5 minutes per side, or until an instant-read thermometer inserted in the center reads

165 degrees F.

9. Assemble the burgers with the ketchup-mayonnaise sauce, tomato slices, and lettuce on toasted buns.

10. Cooking Spray a nonstick skillet, preferably cast iron (or a grill pan), and heat over medium-high heat for 1 to 2 minutes.

11. Cook, flipping once, until an instant-read thermometer registers 155 degrees Fahrenheit (for pork and bison) or 165 degrees Fahrenheit (for beef or chicken), about 4 to 5 minutes per side.

**Nutritional Information** (per serving)

204 Calories

7 grams of fat

32 grams of carbs

5 grams of protein

**Nutritional Profile:**

Diabetes-appropriate, dairy-free, healthy pregnancy, heart-healthy, low sodium, low calorie

**Tips:**

Save this for later. Refrigerate the ketchup-mayonnaise sauce (Step 3) for up to 1 day. To oil a barbecue rack, oil a folded paper towel and rub it over the rack using tongs. Cooking spray should not be used on a hot grill.

**No. 13: Grilled Chicken Sandwiches**

These delicious sandwiches are exactly what you need for lunch. Spread whole wheat buns with lime dressing and then top with grilled chicken and zucchini to make these mouth-watering sandwiches.

**Preparation Time:** 15 Minutes

**Extra Time:** 15 Minutes

**Total Time:** 30 Minutes

**Portions:** 4

**Produced:** 4 Servings

**Ingredients:**

- 1/4 cup fat-free mayonnaise or salad dressing
- 1/2 teaspoon lime or lemon peel, finely shredded
- 1 medium zucchini or yellow summer squash (see tips below) Cut into 1/4-inch-thick pieces lengthwise.
- 3 tablespoons Worcestershire sauce for the chicken
- 4 skinless, boneless chicken breast halves (total weight: 1 to 1-1/4 pounds)
- 4 split and toasted wheat hamburger buns

**Directions:**

1. To make the lime dressing, combine mayonnaise dressing and lime peel in a small bowl.
2. Refrigerate until ready to serve, covered with plastic wrap or foil.
3. Set aside 1 tablespoon of Worcestershire sauce for brushing on zucchini slices.
4. Brush the remaining 2 tablespoons of Worcestershire sauce on all sides of the chicken.
5. Place the chicken on an uncovered grill rack immediately over medium embers.
6. Grill for 12–15 minutes, or until no longer pink (170°F), flipping once halfway through.
7. Grill zucchini slices for the last 6 minutes of the chicken's grilling time, rotating once and grilling until softened and lightly browned.

8. Spread lime dressing on the cut edges of the toasted buns to serve.
9. If desired, cut the zucchini pieces in half crosswise.
10. Place chicken and zucchini pieces on the bottom buns; top with bun tops. This recipe serves four people.

**Nutritional Information** (per serving)
253 Calories
3 grams of fat
27 grams of carbs
31 grams of protein

**Nutritional Profile:**
Diabetes-appropriate, healthy aging, heart-healthy, high protein, low fat, low sodium, low calorie, nut-free

**Tips:**

For added color, use half of a medium zucchini and half of a medium yellow summer squash.

**No. 14: Chipotle Ranch Egg Salad Wraps**

These delicious wraps put a southwest spin on an easy-to-pack egg salad sandwich. Enjoy your lunch with this diabetic-friendly, healthy wrap recipe.

**Preparation Time:** 20 Minutes

**Total Time:** 20 Minutes

**Portions:** 2 Wraps

**Produced:** 2 Servings

**Ingredients:**

- 1/4 medium avocado, peeled and pitted 1/4 hard-cooked eggs, peeled
- 1/3 big green bell peppers, finely chopped
- 1 finely sliced green onion
- 2 tablespoons salad dressing (light ranch or light fiesta ranch)
- 1 teaspoon lime juice
- 1/8 teaspoon of salt
- Dash to one eighth tsp. ground chipotle chili pepper.
- 2 (8-inch) whole wheat tortillas with minimal carbs
- 2 romaine lettuce leaves

**Directions:**

1. Mash the eggs and avocado in a mixing bowl until coarsely mashed.
2. Stir in the remaining six ingredients (chipotle chili pepper).
3. Place the tortillas on a flat surface.
4. Arrange lettuce leaves on top of the tortillas.
5. Fill the bottom third of the tortillas with the egg mixture.
6. Roll up the tortillas by folding in the sides.
7. Just before serving, cut in half.

**Nutritional Information** (per serving)

256 Calories

13 grams of fat

25 grams of carbs

10 grams of protein

**Nutritional Profile:**

Diabetes-appropriate, low-calorie, egg-free, nut-free, soy-free, healthy aging, healthy immunity, vegetarian

**Tips:**

Leave the wraps whole to pack for lunch. Wrap each sandwich in plastic wrap and set it in an insulated lunchbox. Refrigerate the lunchboxes or add cooler packs to them. Consume the wraps within 5 hours.

## No. 15: Zesty Sloppy Joes

This classic gets a healthy kick from your favorite ground beef sandwich when it is combined with jalapeno peppers and chili powder.

**Preparation Time:** 20 Minutes

**Extra Time:** 3 Hours

**Total Time:** 3 Hours, 20 Minutes

**Portions:** 8 Sandwiches

**Produced:** 8 Serving

**Ingredients:**

- 1-1/2 pound lean ground beef (see tips below)
- 1 cup chopped onion
- 1 minced garlic clove
- 1 can (6 oz.) of vegetable juice
- 1/2 cup of ketchup
- 1/2 cup of water
- 2 tablespoons heat-stabilized sugar substitute
- 2 tablespoons chopped canned jalapeno peppers (optional)
- 1 tablespoon Dijon mustard
- 2 tablespoons of chili powder
- 1 teaspoon Worcestershire sauce
- 8 split and toasted whole wheat hamburger buns

- 1 shredded reduced-fat cheddar cheese slice
- 1 huge strip of sweet pepper

**Directions:**

1. Cook the ground beef, onion, and garlic in a large skillet until the meat is brown and the onion is soft. Remove the fat.
2. Meanwhile, add vegetable juice, ketchup, water, sugar substitute, jalapeno peppers (if preferred), mustard, chili powder, and Worcestershire sauce to a 3-1/2 or 4-quart slow cooker. Incorporate the meat mixture.
3. Cook, covered, on low heat for 6 to 8 hours or on high heat for 3 to 4 hours. Fill the bun halves with the meat mixture.
4. Sprinkle with cheese and serve with sweet pepper strips if preferred.

**Nutritional Information** (per serving)

294 Calories

11 grams of fat

30 grams of carbs

20 grams of protein

**Nutritional Profile:**

Diabetes-appropriate, dairy-free, egg-free, healthy pregnancy, heart-healthy, high protein, low sodium, low calorie, and nut-free

**Tips:**

You can substitute lean ground turkey (at least 93 percent lean, or 94 percent) in place of ground beef. Line your slow cooker with a disposable slow cooker liner. Add the ingredients as directed in the recipe. Once your dish is finished cooking, spoon the food out of your slow cooker and simply dispose of the liner.

Note: Avoid lifting or transporting the disposable liner with food inside.

## No. 16: Roast Beef, Arugula, and Pickled Onion Wrap

Making a quick pickle with some onions the night before will help put a delicious twist on your healthy lunch wrap.

**Preparation Time:** 15 Minutes

**Extra Time:** 8 Hours

**Total Time:** 8 Hours, 15 Minutes

**Portions:** 1 Wrap

**Produced:** 1 Serving

**Ingredients:**

- 2 tablespoons of apple cider vinegar
- 1 tablespoon of honey
- 1 teaspoon of salt 1/4 cup finely chopped red onion
- 1 (8-inch) Tumaro's brand low-carb whole wheat flour tortilla
- 2 ounces cooked, thinly sliced, low-sodium roast beef
- 1 tablespoon mango chutney
- 1 cup of arugula

**Directions:**

1. Combine vinegar, honey, and salt in a small bowl.
2. Mix in the onion. Refrigerate overnight.
3. To assemble, spread the chutney over the tortilla and top with the meat and arugula.

4. Remove the onion and discard the juice. Serve the onion over the arugula.
5. Wrap the tortilla tightly around the filling.

**Nutritional Information** (per serving)

239 Calories

5 grams of fat

32 grams of carbs

21 grams of protein

**Nutritional Profile:**

Diabetes-appropriate, dairy-free, egg-free, low-calorie, nut-free, and soy-free

**Tips:**

For a weeknight meal for 4, use 1/2 cup cider vinegar, 1 tablespoon. honey, 1/8 teaspoon. salt, 1 cup onion, 4 tortillas, 1/4 cup chutney, 8 oz. roast beef, and 4 cups arugula.

To pack for lunch, wrap in plastic wrap and pack in an insulated bag with an ice pack.

**No. 17: Beef Brisket in Ale**

The flavorful gravy made from the beer-spiked cooking liquid is the finishing touch to this tender meat dish.

**Preparation Time:** 25 Minutes

**Extra Time:** 10 Hours

**Total Time:** 10 Hours, 25 minutes

**Portions:** 10

**Produced:** 10 Servings

**Ingredients:**

- 3 to 4 lbs. fresh beef brisket
- 2 medium, thinly sliced onions, split into rings
- 1 bay leaf
- 1/4 cup chili sauce 1 (12 fluid ounce) can of beer
- 2 tablespoons heat-stabilized, no-calorie granular sugar alternative
- 1/2 teaspoon dried thyme crushed 1/4 teaspoon of salt, 1/4 teaspoon of black pepper
- 1 minced garlic clove
- 2 teaspoons of cornstarch
- 2 tablespoons ice cold water
- 10 rolls of Italian bread

**Directions:**

1. Remove the fat from the meat. Cut the brisket to suit a 3-1/2 to 6-quart slow cooker if necessary.
2. In the cooker, combine the onions, bay leaf, and brisket.
3. Combine beer, chili sauce, sugar substitute, garlic, thyme, salt, and pepper in a medium mixing bowl; pour over meat.
4. Cook, covered, for 10 to 12 hours on low heat or 5 to 6 hours on high heat.
5. Transfer the brisket and onions to a serving plate and cover with foil to keep warm. Remove the bay leaf.
6. Pour fluids into a large measuring cup for gravy; skim fat.
7. 2-1/2 cups of liquid are measured; the remaining liquid is discarded.
8. In a medium saucepan, combine cornstarch and water; add cooking liquid.

9. Cook and stir for 2 minutes more, or until thickened and bubbling.
10. Serve the meat on bread buns with gravy.

**Nutritional Information** (per serving)

325 Calories

8 grams of fat

35 grams of carbs

25 grams of protein

**Nutritional Profile:**

Diabetes-appropriate, dairy-free, low-calorie, egg-free, nut-free, soy-free, healthy aging, healthy immunity, healthy pregnancy

**Tips:**

For easy cleanup, line your slow cooker with a disposable slow cooker liner. Add the ingredients as directed in the recipe. Once your dish is finished cooking, spoon the food out of your slow cooker and simply dispose of the liner. Avoid lifting or transporting the disposable liner with food inside.

**No. 18: Barbecued Pork Sandwiches**

Making your own barbecue sauce is a far better option than using store-bought commercial sauce, and it lowers the sodium content in this dish.

**Preparation Time:** 20 Minutes

**Extra Time:** 10 Minutes

**Total Time:** 30 Minutes

**Portions:** 6 Sandwiches

**Produced:** 6 servings

**Ingredients:**

- Cooking spray that is nonstick
- 1 medium sliced onion
- 2 minced garlic cloves, 2/3 cup water
- 1/2 (6 oz) can tomato paste (1/3 cup)
- 2 tablespoons of red wine vinegar
- 1 tablespoon brown sugar, packed
- 1-1/2 tsp chili powder
- 1 teaspoon crushed dried oregano
- 1 teaspoon of Worcestershire sauce
- 1/4 teaspoon salt, 12 ounces pork tenderloin
- 1 medium green sweet pepper, thinly sliced
- 6 split and toasted whole wheat hamburger buns

**Directions:**

1. Coat a small, unheated saucepan lightly with nonstick cooking spray.
2. Preheat a medium-sized saucepan over medium heat.
3. Cook and stir the onion and garlic for about 5 minutes, or until the onion is soft.
4. Add the water, tomato paste, vinegar, brown sugar, chili powder, oregano, and Worcestershire sauce and stir to combine.
5. Bring to a boil, then turn off the heat. Cook, uncovered, for about 10 minutes, or until the desired consistency is reached, stirring occasionally.
6. Trim the fat from the meat in the meantime. Cut the meat into small strips.
7. Coat a big, unheated skillet lightly with nonstick cooking spray.
8. Preheat the skillet to medium-high.
9. Season the meat with salt.
10. Cook and stir for 2 to 3 minutes, or until the middle of the meat is

slightly pink.

11. Heat through the sauce and sweet pepper.
12. Serve the meat mixture on toasted hamburger buns.

**Nutritional Information** (per serving)

214 Calories

4 grams of fat

27 grams of carbs

17 grams of protein

**Nutritional Profile:**

Diabetes-appropriate, dairy-free, egg-free, healthy aging, high protein, low sodium, low calorie, and nut-free

**No. 19: Mediterranean Veggie Wrap with Cilantro Hummus**

These healthy multigrain wraps are filled with mixed greens, chopped cucumber, tomato, and red onion, as well as feta cheese and homemade cilantro hummus. To save time, the hummus can be prepared up to 3 days ahead and chilled until you are ready to make the wraps.

**Preparation Time:** 20 Minutes

**Total Time:** 20 Minutes

**Portions:** 4 Wraps

**Produced:** 4 Servings

**Ingredients:**

**Cilantro Hummus**

- 1 peeled garlic clove
- 1 can (15 oz.) of no-salt-added garbanzo beans (chickpeas)
- 3 tablespoons lemon juice
- 2 tablespoons olive oil
- 1 tablespoon tahini (sesame seed paste)
- 1/4 teaspoon of salt
- 1/4 teaspoon white pepper
- 1/4 cup cilantro leaves

## Mediterranean Wraps

- 4 cups baby greens, mixed
- 1/2 large cucumber, halved and sliced (1 cup)
- 1 cup tomato, chopped
- 1/2 cup red onion, thinly sliced
- 1/4 cup crumbled low-fat feta cheese
- 2 tablespoons bottled, sliced mild banana peppers
- 1 tablespoon balsamic vinegar
- 1 tablespoon of olive oil
- 1 minced garlic clove, 1/4 teaspoon black pepper
- 4 (8-inch) oval multigrain wraps with a light tomato flavor

## Directions:

## To Prepare Cilantro Hummus:

1. Drop 1 peeled garlic clove through the feed tube of a food processor fitted with a steel blade attachment and process until finely chopped.
2. Scrape down the bowl's sides.
3. Drain and rinse one 15-ounce can of no-salt-added garbanzo beans (chickpeas).
4. Garbanzo beans, 3 tablespoons lemon juice, 2 tablespoons olive oil, 1 tablespoon tahini (sesame seed paste), 1/4 teaspoon salt, and 1/4

113

teaspoon white pepper are all good additions.

5. Process until completely smooth, scraping down the edges as needed.
6. 1/4 cup of fresh cilantro leaves is optional.
7. Several times, or until the cilantro is equally dispersed and diced, pulse the food processor.
8. Chill until ready to use (see tips below).

**To Prepare Mediterranean Wraps:**

1. Combine the greens, cucumber, tomato, red onion, feta cheese, and banana peppers in a large mixing bowl.
2. In a small mixing bowl, combine the vinegar, olive oil, garlic, and black pepper.
3. The dressing mixture should be poured over the greens mixture. To mix, toss everything together.
4. Spread around 2-1/2 tablespoons of hummus on each wrap.
5. Dressed greens mixture on top.
6. Roll up. Serve right away.

**Nutritional Information** (per serving)
269 Calories
12 grams of fat
35 grams of carbs
16 grams of protein

**Nutritional Profile:**
Diabetes-appropriate, egg-free, healthy aging, healthy immunity, heart-healthy, high fiber, high protein, low sodium, low calorie, nut-free, vegetarian

**Tips:**

Hummus may be prepared and chilled for up to 3 days before use.

## No. 20: Chicken and Cucumber Pita Sandwiches with Yogurt Sauce

If you enjoy eating Greek food, then you will love this healthy Greek-inspired chicken pita recipe. Cucumbers are used twice. They're grated to lend a refreshing flavor to the quick cucumber yogurt sauce and sliced to provide a cool crunch tucked into the pita. Serve these sandwiches for a healthy dinner or light lunch.

**Preparation Time:** 45 Minutes

**Extra Time:** 1 Hour

**Total Time:** 1 Hour, 45 Minutes

**Portions:** 4 Sandwiches

**Produced:** 4 Servings

**Ingredients:**

- 1 tsp. lemon zest
- 2 tablespoons freshly squeezed lemon juice
- 5 teaspoons of olive oil, divided
- 1 teaspoon dried oregano or 1 tablespoon chopped fresh oregano
- 1/4 teaspoon crushed red pepper, split 2-3/4 teaspoons minced garlic
- 1 pound of tender chicken
- 1 halved, seeded, and grated English cucumber, plus 1/2 halves and sliced English cucumber
- 1/2 teaspoon salt (divided)
- 3/4 cup plain, nonfat Greek yogurt
- 2 teaspoons fresh mint, chopped
- 2 teaspoons fresh dill, chopped
- 1 teaspoon of freshly ground pepper

- 2 whole wheat pita flatbreads, halved (6-1/2 inches)
- four lettuce leaves
- 1/2 cup red onion, sliced
- 1 cup plum tomatoes, chopped

**Directions:**

1. In a large mixing bowl, combine lemon zest, lemon juice, 3 teaspoons of oil, oregano, 2 teaspoons of garlic, and crushed red pepper.
2. Toss in the chicken to coat. Marinate for at least 1 hour and up to 4 hours in the refrigerator.
3. Meanwhile, in a fine mesh sieve, combine grated cucumber and 1/4 teaspoon salt.
4. Allow it to drain for 15 minutes before squeezing to release extra liquid.
5. Transfer to a medium mixing bowl. Stir in the yogurt, mint, dill, crushed pepper, the remaining 2 teaspoons of oil, 3/4 teaspoon garlic, and 1/4 teaspoon salt.
6. Place in the refrigerator until ready to serve.
7. Preheat the grill to a medium-high temperature.
8. Oil the grill rack (see below for further information). Grill the chicken for 3 to 4 minutes per side, or until an instant-read thermometer inserted in the center reads 165 degrees F.
9. Spread some of the sauce inside each pita half before serving.
10. Insert the chicken, lettuce, red onion, tomatoes, and cucumber slices.

**Nutritional Information** (per serving)

353 Calories

9 grams of fat

33 grams of carbs

38 grams of protein

**Nutritional Profile:**

Diabetes-appropriate, egg-free, healthy aging, healthy immunity, heart-healthy, high protein, low added sugars, low sodium, low calorie, nut-free, and soy-free

**Tips:**

To oil the grill rack, soak a paper towel with vegetable oil, hold it with tongs, and rub it over the grates. (Do not use cooking spray on a hot grill.)

Plan ahead: Refrigerate yogurt sauce (Step 2) for up to 2 days. For leftover sandwiches, prepare through Step 4, but only assemble what you'll eat immediately.

Store the leftover sauce, sliced vegetables, and grilled chicken separately and assemble just before serving for lunch or dinner the next day.

## No. 21: Open-Face Goat Cheese Sandwich with Tomato and Avocado Salad

This very simple lunch comes together in just 10 minutes, making it a great option for those busy days.

**Preparation Time:** 10 Minutes

**Total Time:** 10 Minutes

**Portions:** 1 Sandwich

**Produced:** 1 Serving

**Ingredients:**

- 1/4 cup halved grape tomatoes
- 1/3 peeled and cubed (or sliced) avocado

- 1/8 teaspoon of salt
- 1/4 cup chopped fresh basil + 2 tablespoons, divided 3/4 ounce soft goat cheese (2 tablespoons)
- 1 toasted large slice of whole wheat bread (1-1/2 ounce)
- 1/8 teaspoon ground pepper
- 1 tablespoon roasted pine nuts (see tips below)
- 1-1/2 tsp extra virgin olive oil
- 1 tablespoon balsamic vinegar

## Directions:

1. In a small bowl, combine the tomatoes, avocado, salt, and 1/4 cup basil.
2. Spread goat cheese on top of the toast.
3. Season with pepper and the remaining 2 tablespoons of basil.
4. Along with the toast, serve the tomato salad.
5. Drizzle with oil and sprinkle with pine nuts.
6. Serve the vinegar on the side.

## Nutritional Information (per serving)

424 Calories

29 grams of fat

33 grams of carbs

13 grams of protein

## Nutritional Profile:

Diabetes-appropriate, egg-free, soy-free, vegetarian

## Tips:

To toast pine nuts, cook them in a small, dry skillet over medium-low heat, stirring constantly, until fragrant, 2 to 4 minutes. Transfer to a small plate and let cool.

## No. 22: Veggie & Hummus Sandwich

This mile-high vegetable and hummus sandwich is the perfect heart-healthy vegetarian lunch to go. Alternatively, you can mix it up with different flavors of hummus and different types of vegetables, if desired.

**Preparation Time:** 10 Minutes

**Total Time:** 10 Minutes

**Portions:** 1

**Produced:** 1 Sandwich

**Ingredients:**

- 2 slices whole wheat bread
- Hummus (3 tablespoons)
- 1/4 avocado (mashed)
- 1/2 cup salad greens, mixed
- 1/4 medium sliced red bell pepper 1/4 cup sliced cucumber
- 1/4 cup carrot shredded

**Directions:**

1. Spread hummus on one slice of bread and avocado on the other.
2. Add greens, bell peppers, cucumbers, and carrots to the sandwich.
3. Cut in half and serve.

**Nutritional Information** (per serving)
325 Calories
14 grams of fat
40 grams of carbs

13 grams of protein

**Nutritional Profile:**

Diabetes-appropriate, dairy-free, egg-free, healthy aging, healthy immunity, healthy pregnancy, heart-healthy, high fiber, low added sugars, low sodium, low calorie, soy-free, vegan, vegetarian

**Tips:**

To prepare ahead of time, prepare the sandwich and refrigerate for up to four hours, or put it in a portable, airtight container with a cooler pack for work or school.

**No. 23: Salmon Pita Sandwich**

Because of the canned sockeye salmon, this quick salmon pita lunch meal is high in heart-healthy omega-3 fatty acids. If you're bringing this sandwich to work, keep the salmon salad separate and stuff the pita only right before eating.

**Cook Time:** 10 Minutes

**Total Time:** 10 Minutes

**Portions:** 1 Sandwich

**Produced:** 1 Serving

**Ingredients:**

- 2 tablespoons plain, nonfat yogurt
- 2 teaspoons fresh dill, chopped; 2 teaspoons lemon juice
- 1/2 teaspoon horseradish, prepared

- 3 ounces of canned flaked sockeye salmon, drained
- One half 6" whole wheat pita bread
- 1/2 cup watercress

## Directions:

1. In a small mixing bowl, combine yogurt, dill, lemon juice, and horseradish; stir in salmon.
2. Fill half of the pita with the salmon salad and watercress.

## Nutritional Information (per serving)

239 Calories

7 grams of fat

19 grams of carbs

25 grams of protein

## Nutritional Profile:

Diabetes-appropriate, bone health, egg-free, healthy aging, healthy pregnancy, heart-healthy, high calcium, high protein, low sodium, low calorie, nut-free, omega-3, soy-free

## No. 24: Cucumber Sandwich

The English cucumber sandwich gets a healthy fiber bump with sprouted whole grain bread. This easy open-face sandwich recipe is a great healthy snack or pack-a-lunch idea.

**Preparation Time:** 5 Minutes

**Total Time:** 5 Minutes

**Portions:** 1 Sandwich

**Produced:** 1 Serving

**Ingredients:**

- 1 whole grain sprouted bread slice
- 1 tablespoon goat cheese
- 1/3 cup of cucumber slices
- Pepper, freshly ground

**Directions:**

1. Garnish the toast with goat cheese and cucumber slices.
2. To taste, season with ground pepper.

**Nutritional Information** (per serving)

125 Calories

4 grams of fat

17 grams of carbs

7 grams of protein

**Nutritional Profile:**

Diabetes-appropriate, heart-healthy, low-calorie, high-fiber, egg-free, low-sodium, nut-free, soy-free, low in added sugars, vegetarian

**No. 25: Roasted Veggies and Hummus Sandwich**

Spruce up your sandwich game with a medley of roasted veggies. If you want extra vegetables throughout the week, roast a whole sheet pan in Step 1, then add the cooked veggies to salads, sandwiches, and pasta dishes, or serve them as a side dish.

**Preparation Time:** 10 Minutes

**Extra Time:** 25 Minutes

**Total Time:** 35 Minutes

**Portions:** 1

**Produced:** 1 Open-face sandwich

**Ingredients:**

- 1/2 cup sliced mixed veggies, such as bell peppers, eggplant, and summer squash (see tips below).
- 1 teaspoon of olive oil
- One 100% whole wheat bread slice
- 2 tablespoon hummus
- 1/2 cup spinach leaves
- 1 teaspoon raw, unsalted sunflower seeds
- 2 chopped fresh basil leaves

**Directions:**

1. Preheat the oven to 350 degrees Fahrenheit.
2. Toss sliced vegetables with olive oil on a small, rimmed baking sheet.
3. Roast for about 25 minutes, or until the vegetables are soft.
4. If desired, toast the bread lightly.
5. Spread hummus on top of the bread.
6. Layer spinach on top, followed by the roasted vegetables.
7. Sprinkle with sunflower seeds and, if preferred, sprinkle with basil.

**Nutritional Information** (per serving)
270 Calories
15 grams of fat
27 grams of carbs

11 grams of protein

**Nutritional Profile:**

Diabetes-appropriate, dairy-free, egg-free, healthy aging, healthy immunity, healthy pregnancy, heart-healthy, high fiber, low added sugars, low sodium, low calorie, nut-free, soy-free, vegan, vegetarian

**Tips:**

Extra veggies can be roasted in Step 1 and refrigerated, covered, for up to 5 days. Microwave on high for 30 seconds to reheat.

**No. 26: Chicken and Cucumber Lettuce Wraps with Peanut Sauce**

You will love the crunch from sliced cucumber and jicama in these savory chicken lettuce wraps. Serve with a simple peanut sauce for an easy lunch recipe that will impress kids and adults alike.

**Preparation Time:** 40 Minutes

**Total Time:** 40 Minutes

**Portions:** 4

**Produced:** 8 Lettuce Wraps

**Ingredients:**

- 1/4 cup smooth peanut butter
- 2 tablespoons of soy sauce (low sodium)
- 2 tablespoons of honey
- 2 tablespoons of water
- 2 teaspoons sesame oil, roasted

- 2 teaspoons olive oil
- 3 sliced onions, white and green sections separated
- 2 teaspoons serrano pepper, seeded and minced
- 1 tablespoon fresh ginger, minced
- 2 teaspoons fresh minced garlic
- 1 pound of chicken breast ground
- 1 cup jicama, diced
- 16 leaves of Bibb lettuce
- 1 cup brown rice, cooked
- 1 cup English cucumber, halved and thinly sliced
- 1/2 cup cilantro leaves
- For serving, lime wedges

## Directions:

1. In a small mixing bowl, combine the peanut butter, soy sauce, honey, water, and sesame oil.
2. In a large nonstick skillet over medium heat, heat the olive oil.
3. Cook until the scallions whites, serrano, ginger, and garlic begin to soften, about 2 minutes.
4. Cook, breaking up the chicken with a spoon or potato masher, until cooked through, 3 to 4 minutes.
5. Cook until the peanut sauce has thickened, about 3 minutes, in the chicken mixture.
6. Take the pan off the heat.
7. Mix in the jicama and scallions greens.
8. Make 8 stacks of 2 lettuce leaves each to serve.
9. Divide the lettuce cups with the rice, chicken mixture, cucumber, and cilantro.
10. Serve with wedges of lime.

## Nutritional Information (per serving)
521 Calories

26 grams of fat

44 grams of carbs

34 grams of protein

**Nutritional Profile:**

Diabetes-appropriate, bone health, dairy-free, egg-free, healthy aging, healthy immunity, healthy pregnancy, heart-healthy, high blood pressure, high calcium, high fiber, high protein, low sodium, low calorie

**Tips:**

To make ahead of time, assemble the lettuce wraps and refrigerate for up to four hours, or put them in a portable, airtight container with a cooler pack for work or school.

**No. 27: Turkey Apple Brie Sandwiches**

These hollowed-out baguettes hold a satisfying combo of tart apples, creamy Brie, and protein-rich shredded turkey.

**Preparation Time:** 20 Minutes

**Total Time:** 20 Minutes

**Portions:** 4 Sandwiches

**Produced:** 4 Servings

**Ingredients:**

- 1 finely sliced Granny Smith apple
- 1 teaspoon of lemon juice
- 8 ounces of whole wheat baguette

- 4 red-leaf lettuce leaves
- 1 cup shredded cooked turkey breast (4 ounces) (see tips below)
- 2 ounces of finely sliced Brie cheese
- 4 teaspoons of Dijon mustard

## Directions:

1. In a small bowl, combine apple slices and lemon juice.
2. Cut the baguette into four halves crosswise.
3. Each portion should be cut in half lengthwise.
4. Remove the bread's soft interior core, leaving a 1/4-inch-thick shell. (Keep the interior bread for another purpose.)
5. Add lettuce, turkey, brie, and apple slices to the bottom pieces of bread.
6. Spread mustard on the tops of the sandwiches and place one on each.
7. Serve right away, or wrap and chill for up to 4 hours.

## Nutritional Information (per serving)

236 Calories

5 grams of fat

32 grams of carbs

17 grams of protein

## Nutritional Profile:

Diabetes-appropriate, low-calorie, egg-free, nut-free, and soy-free, healthy aging

## Tips:

To cook turkey, place 1 turkey breast tenderloin in a skillet with 1 cup water. Bring to a boil. Reduce heat, cover, and simmer until the internal temperature reaches 165 degrees Fahrenheit, 20 to 25 minutes. Remove it from the pan. When cool enough to handle, shred with two forks. Refrigerate any remaining turkey in an airtight container for up to 3 days or freeze for up to 2 months.

## No. 28: Spicy Tuna Salad English Muffin Sandwich

This simple, quick lunch idea has a delicious balance of flavors. A bit of a spicy Sriracha-mayonnaise mixture adds heat to the tuna salad, while the quick pickled cucumbers provide brightness. Helpful tip: Make sure to toast the English muffin so the sandwich doesn't get soggy.

**Preparation Time:** 10 Minutes

**Total Time:** 10 Minutes

**Portions:** 1 Sandwich

**Ingredients:**

- 1 teaspoon of rice vinegar
- 1/2 teaspoon soy sauce (low sodium)
- 1/4 teaspoon honey
- 1/4 cup English cucumber, thinly sliced
- 1 teaspoon of mayonnaise
- 1 tablespoon scallion, thinly sliced
- 1/2 teaspoon . Sriracha or other hot sauce
- 1/2 teaspoon sesame oil, toasted
- Optional: a pinch of crushed red pepper
- 2-1/2 oz. no-salt-added water-drained, packed canned tuna
- 1 whole wheat English muffin, toasted

**Directions:**

1. In a small mixing bowl, combine the vinegar, soy sauce, and honey.
2. Toss in the cucumber slices to coat. Set aside.
3. In a separate small bowl, combine the mayonnaise, scallions, Sriracha (or other hot sauce if desired), sesame oil, and crushed red pepper, if

using.

4. Stir in the tuna.
5. Cucumbers should be drained.
6. Top each muffin half with the tuna mixture and cucumbers.
7. Cover the second half of the muffin.

## Nutritional Information (per serving)

349 Calories

15 grams of fat

31 grams of carbs

24 grams of protein

## Nutritional Profile:

Diabetes-appropriate, dairy-free, heart-healthy, high-protein, and nut-free

## No. 29: White Bean and Veggie Salad

This meatless lunch dish salad combines creamy, satisfying white beans and avocado. Try mixing it up with different seasonal vegetables.

**Preparation Time:** 10 Minutes

**Total Time:** 10 Minutes

**Portions:** 1

**Produced:** 4 cups

## Ingredients:

- 2 cups salad greens, mixed
- 3/4 cup chopped vegetables of your choice, such as cucumbers and cherry tomatoes

- 1/3 cup rinsed and drained canned white beans
- 1/2 diced avocado
- 1 tablespoon red-wine vinegar
- 2 teaspoons of extra-virgin olive oil
- 1/4 teaspoon of kosher salt
- To taste, freshly ground pepper

## Directions:

1. In a medium mixing bowl, combine the greens, vegetables, beans, and avocado.
2. Season with salt and pepper, and drizzle with vinegar and oil.
3. Toss everything together and transfer it to a large plate.

## Nutritional Information (per serving)

360 Calories

25 grams of fat

30 grams of carbs

10 grams of protein

## Nutritional Profile:

Diabetes-appropriate, dairy-free, egg-free, gluten-free, healthy pregnancy, high fiber, low calorie, nut-free, soy-free, vegan, vegetarian

## Tips:

Feel free to use your favorite vegetables or whatever you have on hand, like bell peppers, radishes, or celery. Try mixing it up with different seasonal vegetables. If you have leftover roasted vegetables, make sure they are cooled completely before adding them to the salad.

## No. 30: Chipotle Orange Broccoli & Tofu

I love having stir-fries, and the chipotle peppers added to this recipe give a kick to this tofu and broccoli stir-fry recipe. If you're shy about spices, cut back on the amount or leave them out completely if desired. Serve over brown basmati rice.

**Cook Time:** 30 Minutes

**Total Time:** 30 Minutes

**Portions:** 4

**Produced:** 4 Servings

**Ingredients:**

- One 14-oz. package of extra-firm, water-packed tofu
- 1/2 teaspoon of salt, 3 tablespoons of canola oil, and 6 cups of broccoli florets
- 1 cup of orange juice
- 1 tablespoon chipotle in adobo chopped (see tips below), seeded if desired
- 1/2 cup fresh cilantro, chopped

**Directions:**

1. Tofu should be drained and patted dry before cutting into 1/2- to 3/4-inch pieces.
2. 1/4 teaspoon of salt should be sprinkled on all sides of the tofu.
3. In a large nonstick skillet over medium-high heat, heat 2 tablespoons of oil.
4. Cook, stirring every couple of minutes, until the tofu is golden brown, 7 to 9 minutes total. Place on a platter.
5. Add the remaining 1 tablespoon oil and broccoli to the skillet, along with the remaining 1/4 teaspoon of salt; cook, stirring constantly, for 1

minute, or until the broccoli is bright green.

6. Cook, tossing constantly, until the broccoli is barely cooked, 2 to 3 minutes more.

7. Replace the tofu in the pan. 1 to 2 minutes, gently tossing, until the tofu is heated through.

8. Take the pan off the heat and whisk in the cilantro.

**Nutritional Information** (per serving)

242 Calories

17 grams of fat

14 grams of carbs

14 grams of protein

**Nutritional Profile:**

Diabetes-appropriate, dairy-free, bone health, healthy aging, healthy immunity, heart health, high calcium, low added sugars, low carbohydrate, low sodium, low calorie, vegan, vegetarian

**Tips:**

Look for the small cans of chipotle chiles in adobo sauce with Mexican foods at large supermarkets.

**In Summary:**

This is far from a comprehensive list of type 2 diabetes lunch recipes. I've experimented with these recipes many times over the years, mixing and matching, and I encourage you to do the same. Make these lunch recipes to fit your specific needs.

In addition, I recommend that you use these lunch recipes to plan your meals with the planners that I have included. Enjoy!

# 8

# Dinner Recipes

Some of these amazing healthy dishes will blow your taste buds away and help you accomplish your diabetic goals. These delectable meals range from creamy soups to fiery tacos, with plenty of tempting options in between.

These meals will spice up your evening routine while sticking to your eating pattern, with lower saturated fat and sodium levels and a concentration on complex carbs, such as whole grains, particularly for type 2 diabetics.

Mouth-watering recipes like Slow Cooker Braised Beef with Carrots and Turnips and Chicken and Spinach Skillet Pasta with Lemon and Parmesan are very satisfying ways to end your day.

## No. 1: Chicken & Spinach Skillet Pasta with Lemon

This one-pan chicken pasta combines lean chicken breast and sauteed spinach for a one-bowl meal that is garlicky, lemony, and best served with a little Parmesan on top. It's a quick and easy weeknight dinner the whole family will love.

**Preparation Time:** 25 Minutes

**Overall Time:** 25 Minutes

**Portions:** 4

**Produced:** 4 Servings

**Ingredients:**

- 8 oz. gluten-free penne or whole wheat penne pasta
- 2 tablespoons extra-virgin olive oil
- 1 pound boneless, skinless chicken breast or thighs, trimmed and chopped into bite-size pieces if necessary.
- 1/2 teaspoon salt
- 1/4 teaspoon black pepper
- 4 minced garlic cloves
- 1/2 cup white wine, dry
- 1 lemon, juice, and zest
- 10 cups fresh spinach, chopped
- 4 tablespoons grated Parmesan cheese (divided)

**Directions:**

1. Cook the pasta as directed on the packet. Set aside after draining.
2. Meanwhile, in a large, high-sided skillet over medium-high heat, heat the oil.
3. Stir in the chicken, salt, and pepper until it is just cooked through, 5 to 7 minutes.
4. Cook, stirring constantly, until the garlic is aromatic, about 1 minute.
5. Bring to a simmer with the wine, lemon juice, and zest.
6. Take the pan off the heat. Incorporate the spinach and cooked pasta.
7. Cover and let stand until the spinach is barely wilted.
8. Divide among four servings and top with 1 tbsp. Parmesan.

**Nutritional Information** (per serving)

   335 Calories

   12 grams of fat

   25 grams of carbs

   29 grams of protein

**Nutritional Profile:**

   Diabetes-appropriate, egg-free, gluten-free, healthy aging, healthy immunity, heart-healthy, high protein, low sodium, low calorie, nut-free, and soy-free

### No. 2: Slow-Cooker Braised Beef with Carrots and Turnips

The spice blend in this healthy beef stew recipe—cinnamon, allspice, and cloves—may bring up images of apple pie, but this combo is also a great fit in savory applications too. Serve over creamy polenta or buttered whole wheat egg noodles, if desired.

**Cook Time:** 40 Minutes

**Additional Time:** 3 Hours, 20 Minutes

**Overall Time:** 4 Hours

**Portions:** 8

**Produced:** 8 Servings

**Ingredients:**

- 1 tablespoon of kosher salt
- 2 teaspoons cinnamon powder
- 1/2 teaspoon allspice powder

- 1/2 teaspoon ground pepper 1/4 teaspoon ground cloves
- Three 3-1/2 pounds of trimmed beef chuck roast
- 2 tbsp. extra-virgin olive oil
- 1 medium sliced onion
- 3 garlic cloves, sliced
- 1 cup of red wine
- 1 can (28 oz.) of whole tomatoes, ideally San Marzano
- 5 medium carrots, peeled and chopped into 1-inch chunks
- 2 medium peeled and cut into 1/2-inch pieces of turnips
- Garnish with chopped fresh basil.

**Equipment:** 5 to 6-quart slow cooker

**Directions:**

1. In a small bowl, combine the salt, cinnamon, allspice, pepper, and cloves. Apply the mixture to the beef all over.
2. In a large skillet over medium heat, heat the oil.
3. Cook until the steak is browned, 4 to 5 minutes per side.
4. Fill a 5- to 6-quart slow cooker halfway with water.
5. In the pan, add the onion and garlic. Cook, stirring constantly, for 2 minutes.
6. Bring the wine and tomatoes (with juice) to a boil, scraping away any browned parts and breaking up the tomatoes as you go.
7. Combine the mixture with the carrots and turnips in the slow cooker.
8. Cook on high for 4 hours or low for 8 hours, covered.
9. Remove the steak from the slow cooker and cut it into slices.
10. Serve the beef with the sauce and veggies, if preferred, garnished with basil.

**Nutritional Information** (per serving)
318 Calories
11 grams of fat

13 grams of carbs

35 grams of protein

## Nutritional Profile:

Diabetes-appropriate, dairy-free, egg-free, gluten-free, healthy aging, healthy immunity, healthy pregnancy, heart-healthy, high protein, low added sugars, low carbohydrate, low sodium, low calorie, nut-free, and soy-free

## Tips:

40 minutes Slow cooker time: 4 to 8 hours

Make ahead of time: Refrigerate the browned beef (Steps 1 and 2) and tomato mixture (Step 3) separately for up to 1 day. Bring the tomato mixture to a boil before adding it to the slow cooker.

## No. 3: Cream of Turkey and Wild Rice Soup

Check your fridge for leftover chicken or turkey; it goes great with soup! This low-sodium soup recipe is a healthier twist on a classic creamy turkey and wild rice soup that hails from Minnesota. Serve with a crisp romaine salad and whole-grain bread.

**Cook Time:** 35 Minutes

**Overall Time:** 35 Minutes

**Portions:** 4

**Produced:** 4 Servings, about 1 to 3 cups each.

**Ingredients:**

- 1 tablespoon olive oil (extra virgin)
- 2 cups sliced mushrooms (about 4 ounces)
- 3/4 cup chopped celery, 3/4 cup carrots
- 1/4 cup shallots, chopped
- 1/4 cup all-purpose flour, 1/4 teaspoon salt
- 1/4 teaspoon freshly ground pepper
- 4 cups low-sodium chicken broth
- 1 cup quick-cooking or instant wild rice (see the notice about ingredients below)
- 3 cups cooked shredded chicken or turkey (12 oz; see tips below)
- 1/2 cup low-fat sour cream
- 2 tablespoons fresh parsley chopped

## Directions:

1. In a large saucepan over medium heat, heat the oil.
2. Cook, stirring constantly, until the mushrooms, celery, carrots, and shallots are cooked, about 5 minutes.
3. Cook, stirring, for 2 minutes more after adding the flour, salt, and pepper.
4. Bring the broth to a boil, scraping away any browned bits.
5. Reduce the heat to a simmer and add the rice.
6. Cook, covered, for 5 to 7 minutes, or until the rice is soft.
7. Cook until the turkey (or chicken), sour cream, and parsley are cooked thoroughly, about 2 minutes longer.

## Nutritional Information (per serving)

378 Calories

11 grams of fat

29 grams of carbs

37 grams of protein

## Nutritional Profile:

Diabetes-appropriate, healthy aging, healthy immunity, heart-healthy, high protein, low added sugars, low sodium, low calorie

**Tips:**

To poach chicken breasts, place boneless, skinless chicken breasts in a medium skillet or saucepan. Add lightly salted water to cover and bring to a boil. Cover, reduce heat to low, and simmer gently until the chicken is cooked through and no longer pink in the middle, 10 to 12 minutes.

**Ingredient note:** Quick-cooking or instant wild rice has been parboiled to reduce the cooking time. Conventional wild rice takes 40 to 50 minutes to cook. Be sure to check the cooking directions when selecting your rice; some brands labeled "quick" take about 30 minutes to cook. If you can't find the quick-cooking variety, just add cooked conventional wild rice along with the turkey at the end of Step 2.

**No. 4: Green Goddess Salad with Chickpeas**

With this cucumber, tomato, Swiss cheese, and chickpea salad recipe, a healthy green goddess dressing is made from avocado, buttermilk, and herbs. The extra salad dressing is deliciously served with grilled vegetables.

**Preparation Time:** 15 Minutes

**Overall Time:** 15 Minutes

**Portions:** 2

**Produced:** 2 Servings

**Ingredients:**

**To Make The Dressing**

- 1 peeled and pitted avocado
- 1-1/2 cups buttermilk
- 1/4 cup fresh herbs, chopped, such as tarragon, sorrel, mint, parsley, and/or cilantro
- 2 tablespoons of rice vinegar
- 1/2 teaspoon of salt

**To Make The Salad**

- 3 cups romaine lettuce, chopped
- 1 cup of cucumber slices
- 1 (15-ounce) can of rinsed chickpeas 1/4 cup chopped low-fat Swiss cheese
- 6 cherry tomatoes, cut in half if desired

**Directions:**

1. In a blender, combine the avocado, buttermilk, herbs, vinegar, and salt to make the dressing. Blend until smooth.
2. To make the salad, combine the lettuce and cucumber in a mixing bowl with 1/4 cup of the dressing.
3. Chickpeas, cheese, and tomatoes go on top. (The surplus dressing can be refrigerated for up to 3 days.)

**Nutritional Information** (per serving)
304 Calories
8 grams of fat
40 grams of carbs
22 grams of protein

**Nutritional Profile:**

Diabetes-appropriate, bone health, egg-free, gluten-free, healthy aging, healthy immunity, healthy pregnancy, heart-healthy, high calcium, high fiber, high protein, low added sugars, low sodium, low calorie, nut-free, soy-free, vegetarian

**Tips:**

Cover and refrigerate any remaining dressing for up to 3 days.

### No. 5: Ginger Tahini Oven Baked Salmon and Vegetables

I love that the tahini sauce is used twice in this healthy salmon recipe, serving as a glaze for the fish and also as a drizzle for the entire dish at the end of cooking. The green beans are cooked just slightly in this recipe to still be crisp.

If you like your green beans tenderer, look for thinner beans or haricot verts in the grocery store; they will cook a lot faster. This easy sheet pan dinner recipe is not only delicious; it also comes together with just 25 minutes of active prep time, and there is only one pan to clean up afterward!

**Preparation Time:** 25 Minutes

**Additional Time:** 25 Minutes

**Overall Time:** 50 Minutes

**Portions:** 4

**Produced:** 4 Servings

**Ingredients:**

- 1 large cubed sweet potato (approximately 12 ounces)
- 6 cups 1 pound of white button or cremini mushrooms, chopped into 1-inch pieces
- 1/2 teaspoon salt, divided into 2 tablespoons of olive oil
- 1 pound of trimmed green beans
- 2 tablespoons of low-sodium soy sauce
- 1 tablespoon plus 2 teaspoons of tahini
- 1 tablespoon + 1 teaspoon honey
- 1/2 teaspoon fresh ginger, coarsely grated
- 1/4 pound of fish, preferably wild-caught, split into four pieces
- 2 teaspoons of rice vinegar
- 2 tablespoons of fresh chives, chopped (optional)

**Directions:**

1. Preheat the oven to 350°F and prepare a large rimmed baking sheet.
2. Place one rack in the center of the oven and another 6 inches from the broiler. Preheat the oven to 425°F.
3. In a large mixing bowl, combine the sweet potato, mushrooms, 1 tablespoon oil, and 1/4 teaspoon salt; toss to coat.
4. Take the baking sheet out of the oven. Spread the vegetable mixture in an equal layer on the pan and roast for 20 minutes, turning once, until the sweet potatoes begin to brown.
5. Meanwhile, combine the green beans with the remaining 1 tablespoon oil and 1/4 teaspoon salt. In a small bowl, combine the soy sauce, tahini, honey, and ginger.
6. Take the pan out of the oven. Place the mushrooms and sweet potatoes on one side of the pan and the green beans on the other.
7. Place the salmon in the center, nestling it if necessary on top of the vegetables.
8. Half of the tahini sauce should be spread on top of the fish.
9. 8 to 10 minutes more, or until the salmon flakes.
10. Turn the broiler to high, transfer the pan to the top rack, and broil for 3

minutes, or until the salmon is glazed.

11. Drizzle the fish and vegetables with the leftover tahini sauce and vinegar.
12. If preferred, garnish with chives and serve.

**Nutritional Information** (per serving)

555 Calories

30 grams of fat

37 grams of carbs

38 grams of protein

**Nutritional Profile:**

Diabetes-appropriate, dairy-free, egg-free, high protein, low calorie,nut-free, omega-3

**Tips:**

Prepare tahini sauce (Step 4) up to 1 day ahead; cover and refrigerate; save it until ready to use.

**No. 6: Sheet Pan Chicken Fajita Bowls**

Alternatively, you can skip the tortillas in favor of this warm fajita salad, which features a nutritious medley of chicken with roasted kale, bell peppers, and black beans. The chicken, beans, and vegetables are all cooked in the same pan, so this healthy, diabetic-friendly dinner is easy to make, and the cleanup is easy as well.

**Preparation Time:** 20 Minutes

**Additional Time:** 20 Minutes

**Overall Time:** 40 Minutes

**Portions:** 4

**Produced:** 4 Servings

**Ingredients:**

- 2 teaspoons of chili powder
- 2 teaspoons of cumin powder
- 3/4 teaspoon salt, divided
- 1/2 teaspoon of garlic powder
- 1/2 teaspoon of smoked paprika
- 1/4 teaspoon of black pepper
- Divided 2 tablespoons of olive oil.
- 1-1/4 pound chicken tenders
- 4 cups chopped, stemmed kale 1 medium yellow onion, sliced 1 medium red bell pepper, sliced 1 medium green bell pepper, sliced
- 1 (15-ounce) can of drained black beans, no salt added
- 1/4 cup plain, low-fat Greek yogurt
- 1 tablespoon of lime juice
- 2 teaspoons of water

**Directions:**

1. Preheat the oven to 425°F and place a big, rimmed baking sheet in it.
2. Combine chili powder, cumin, 1/2 teaspoon salt, garlic powder, paprika, and ground pepper in a large mixing bowl.
3. Set aside 1 teaspoon of the spice mixture in a medium bowl.
4. In a large mixing bowl, combine 1 tablespoon of oil with the entire spice combination.
5. Toss in the chicken, onion, and red and green bell peppers to coat.
6. Spray the pan with cooking spray after it has been removed from the oven.
7. Spread the chicken mixture evenly on the pan. 15 minutes in the oven

8. Meanwhile, stir the kale and black beans with the remaining 1/4 teaspoon of salt and 1 tablespoon olive oil in a large mixing bowl.
9. Take the pan out of the oven.
10. Combine the chicken and vegetables in a mixing bowl.
11. Distribute the greens and beans equally over top.
12. 5 to 7 minutes more, or until the chicken is cooked through and the vegetables are soft.

**Nutritional Information** (per serving)
343 Calories
10 grams of fat
24 grams of carbs
43 grams of protein

**Nutritional Profile:**
Diabetes-appropriate, egg-free, gluten-free, healthy aging, healthy immunity, healthy pregnancy, high fiber, high protein, low calorie, nut-free, and soy-free

**Tips:**

For easier weeknight prep, slice vegetables the night before, cover, and refrigerate. Prepare the spice mixture (Step 1) up to 2 days ahead; store in an airtight container.

**No. 7: Vegan White Bean Chili**

Fresh Anaheim or poblano chiles add mild heat to this classic white bean chili and contribute tons of smoky flavor. Quinoa adds body to the chili, while diced zucchini provides pretty flecks of green and increases your veggie count for the rest of your day.

**Preparation Time:** 35 Minutes

**Additional Time:** 30 Minutes

**Overall Time:** 1 Hour, 5 Minutes

**Portions:** 6

**Produced:** 6 Servings

**Ingredients:**

- 1/4 cup canola or avocado oil
- 2 cups seeded Anaheim or poblano chilies, diced (about 3)
- 1 big sliced onion
- 4 minced garlic cloves
- 1/2 cup washed quinoa
- 4 teaspoons of dried oregano
- 4 teaspoons of cumin powder
- 1/2 teaspoon powdered coriander 1 teaspoon of salt
- 1/2 teaspoon black pepper
- 4 cups vegetable broth (low sodium)
- 2 (15-ounce) cans of washed white beans, no salt added
- 1 large chopped zucchini (approximately 3 cups)
- 1/4 cup fresh cilantro, chopped
- 2 tablespoons lime juice, plus serving wedges

**Directions:**

1. In a big pot, heat the oil over medium heat.
2. Stir in the chilies, onions, and garlic.
3. Cook, stirring constantly, for 5 to 7 minutes, or until the veggies are softened.
4. Cook, stirring constantly, until the quinoa, oregano, cumin, salt, coriander, and pepper are fragrant, about 1 minute.

5. Combine the broth and beans in a mixing bowl. Bring the water to a boil. Reduce the heat to a low setting.
6. Cook, partially covered, for 20 minutes, stirring periodically.
7. Cook, covered, for 10 to 15 minutes more, or until the zucchini is tender and the chili has thickened.
8. Combine the cilantro and lime juice in a mixing bowl. If desired, garnish with lime wedges.

**Nutritional Information** (per serving)

283 Calories

12 grams of fat

37 grams of carbs

10 grams of protein

**Nutritional Profile:**

Diabetes-appropriate, dairy-free, egg-free, gluten-free, heart-healthy, healthy aging, low-calorie, high-fiber, low-sodium, nut-free, soy-free, vegan, vegetarian

**Tips:**

Refrigerate chili for up to 4 days. Reheat before serving.

**No. 8: Creamy Fettuccine with Brussels Sprouts and Mushrooms**

Brussels sprouts and mushrooms sliced. This fall version of pasta primavera cooks fast and clings to the pasta. Look for presliced mushrooms to reduce prep time. Serve alongside a tossed salad.

**Preparation Time:** 30 Minutes

**Overall Time:** 30 Minutes

**Portions:** 6 People

**Produced:** 6 Servings, about 1-1/2 cups each.

**Ingredients:**

- 12 oz. whole wheat fettuccine
- 1 tablespoon olive oil (extra virgin)
- 4 cups sliced mixed mushrooms (cremini, oyster, or shiitake)
- 4 cups of Brussels sprouts, thinly sliced
- 1 tablespoon of minced garlic
- 1/2 cup dry sherry (see tips below) or 2 tablespoons of sherry vinegar
- 2 cups of nonfat milk
- 2 tablespoons of all-purpose flour
- 1/2 teaspoon of salt
- 1/2 teaspoon of freshly ground pepper
- 1 cup finely shredded Asiago cheese, plus more for garnish

**Directions:**

1. Cook pasta in a large saucepan of boiling water for 8 to 10 minutes, or until tender.
2. Return to the pot and set aside after draining.
3. Meanwhile, in a large skillet over medium heat, heat the oil.
4. Add the mushrooms and Brussels sprouts and simmer, stirring frequently, for 8 to 10 minutes, or until the mushrooms release their liquid.
5. Cook, stirring constantly, until the garlic is aromatic, about 1 minute.
6. Scrape up any brown parts before adding sherry (or vinegar); bring to a boil and simmer, stirring, until almost evaporated, 10 seconds (if using vinegar) or about 1 minute (if using sherry).
7. In a mixing bowl, combine the milk and flour; season with salt and pepper.
8. Cook, stirring constantly, for about 2 minutes, or until the sauce bubbles

and thickens.

9. Melt the asiago by stirring it in.
10. Gently mix the pasta in the sauce.
11. If desired, top with more cheese.

**Nutritional Information** (per serving)

384 Calories

10 grams of fat

56 grams of carbs

18 grams of protein

**Nutritional Profile:**

Diabetes-appropriate, bone health, healthy aging, heart health, high calcium, high fiber, high protein, low added sugars, low sodium, low calorie, vegetarian

**Tips:**

If you prefer dry sherry, it is usually sold with other fortified wines in your wine or liquor store instead of higher-sodium "cooking" sherry.

**No. 9: Loaded Black Bean Nacho Soup**

Spruce up a can of black bean soup with your favorite nacho toppings, such as cheese, avocado, and fresh tomatoes. A bit of smoked paprika adds a bold flavor kick, but you can give it a kick with any warm spices you prefer, such as cumin or chili powder. Look for a soup that contains no more than 450 mg of sodium per serving.

**Preparation Time:** 10 Minutes

**Overall Time:** 10 Minutes

**Portions:** 2

**Produced:** 2 Servings

**Ingredients:**

- 1 carton (18 ounces.) of low-sodium black bean soup
- 1/4 teaspoon of smoked paprika
- 1/2 teaspoon of lime juice
- 1/2 cup grape tomatoes, halved
- 1/2 cup shredded cabbage or cabbage combination
- 2 tablespoons of cotija cheese crumbles or other Mexican-style shredded cheese
- 1/2 medium diced avocado
- 2 ounces of cooked tortilla chips

**Directions:**

1. In a small saucepan, combine the soup and paprika.
2. Heat according to package instructions.
3. Mix in the lime juice.
4. Serve the soup in two bowls, topped with tomatoes, cabbage (or slaw), cheese, and avocado.
5. With tortilla chips, serve.

**Nutritional Information** (per serving)
350 Calories
17 grams of fat
44 grams of carbs
10 grams of protein

**Nutritional Profile:**
Diabetes-appropriate, heart-healthy, healthy aging, high fiber, low added sugars, low sodium, low calories

## No. 10: Roast Chicken and Sweet Potato

This nutritious chicken and sweet potato recipe is a tasty and dependable dinner option. It's a low-calorie sheet-pan dinner that is made with chicken thighs and sweet potatoes and cooks quickly in a hot oven. Serve with a mixed green, apple, and blue cheese salad.

**Cook Time:** 15 Minutes

**Additional Time:** 30 Minutes

**Overall Time:** 45 Minutes

**Portions:** 4

**Produced:** 4 Servings

**Ingredients:**

- 2 tablespoons of whole grain mustard or Dijon mustard
- 2 tablespoons of fresh chopped thyme or 2 teaspoons dried
- 2 tablespoons of extra virgin olive oil, 1/2 teaspoon salt, 1/2 teaspoon freshly ground pepper, divided
- 1-1/2 to 2 pounds bone-in chicken thighs, skin removed
- 2 medium peeled and cut into 1-inch pieces sweet potatoes
- 1 large red onion, peeled and sliced into 1-inch wedges

**Directions:**

1. Preheat the oven to 450°F with the rack in the bottom third position.
2. Preheat a large, rimmed baking sheet in the oven.
3. In a small dish, combine mustard, thyme, 1 tablespoon oil, and 1/4 teaspoon salt and pepper; pour the mixture evenly over the chicken.

151

4. In a mixing bowl, combine the sweet potatoes and onion with the remaining 1 tablespoon of oil and 1/4 teaspoon each of salt and pepper.
5. Remove the baking sheet from the oven with care and distribute the vegetables on it.
6. On top of the vegetables, place the chicken.
7. Return the pan to the oven and roast, tossing once halfway through, for 30 to 35 minutes, or until the veggies are soft and beginning to brown and an instant-read thermometer inserted into a chicken thigh registers 165 degrees Fahrenheit.

**Nutritional Information** (per serving)

408 Calories

17 grams of fat

34 grams of carbs

27 grams of protein

**Nutritional Profile:**

Diabetes-appropriate, dairy-free, gluten-free, healthy aging, healthy immunity, heart-healthy, high protein, low added sugars, low sodium, low calorie

**Tips:**

Reduce the number of dishes you have to wash. A rimmed baking sheet is perfect for everything from roasting to capturing inadvertent drips and spills. For effortless cleanup and to keep your baking sheets in tip-top shape, line them with a layer of foil before each use.

**No. 11: Lemon Chicken and Whole Grain Rice**

This is a really easy Persian-inspired chicken and whole-grain rice dish with a beautiful golden color and a wonderful fragrance. If you have saffron in your cupboard, add that optional pinch; just a little will enhance the flavor and aroma of the dish.

**Preparation Time:** 50 Minutes

**Additional Time:** 45 Minutes

**Overall Time:** 1 Hour, 35 Minutes

**Portions:** 8

**Produced:** 8 Servings

**Ingredients:**

- 2 tablespoons of olive oil, 8 boneless, skinless chicken thighs (1-1/4 to 1-1/2 pounds total), 2 big onions, thinly sliced, 1/2 teaspoon salt, divided
- 3 minced garlic cloves
- 2 teaspoons of turmeric powder
- 1 paprika teaspoon
- 1 large pinch of saffron
- 3 cups shredded cabbage (about 1/2 tiny head)
- 4 cups cooked brown rice (basmati or jasmine preferred)
- 1/4 cup of fresh lemon juice
- 2 tablespoons of fresh Italian parsley, chopped (optional)
- 1 sliced lemon (optional)

**Equipment:** Two 8-inch square baking dishes or foil pans

**Directions:**

1. Preheat the oven to 375 degrees Fahrenheit.
2. Spray two 8-inch square baking dishes or foil pans (see tips below).
3. In a large nonstick skillet over medium-high heat, heat 1 tablespoon of oil.
4. Cook, rotating once, until both sides of the chicken thighs are lightly

browned, about 4 minutes.

5. Place the chicken on a platter and set it aside. Repeat with the rest of the chicken thighs. Pour out all but roughly 1 tablespoon of grease from the pan.

6. Add the remaining 1 tablespoon oil and onions to the pan, along with 1/4 teaspoon salt. Cook, stirring occasionally, for 12 to 15 minutes, or until soft and brown.

7. Stir in the garlic, turmeric, paprika, and saffron, if using (optional); simmer, stirring, for 2 minutes. Put the onions on a platter and set them aside.

8. Bring the pan back up to medium-high heat and add the cabbage.

9. Cook, stirring constantly, for 3 minutes, or until wilted.

10. Stir in the rice, lemon juice, 1/4 teaspoon salt, and half of the reserved onion.

11. Cook for 5 to 7 minutes, or until the whole grain rice is well covered and warm.

12. Divide the rice mixture among the prepared baking plates and top with four of the saved chicken thighs.

13. Half of the leftover fried onions should be placed on top of each. Wrap both dishes in foil, name one, and place it in the freezer for up to a month.

14. Cover and bake the remaining casserole for 30 minutes.

15. Uncover and bake for 5 to 10 minutes more, or until a thermometer inserted into the thickest part of the chicken registers 165 degrees Fahrenheit and the onions begin to brown around the edges.

16. If preferred, garnish with parsley and lemon slices.

**Nutritional Information:** (Per Serving)

274 Calories

10 grams of fat

29 grams of carbs

17 grams of protein

**Nutritional Profile:**

Diabetes-appropriate, dairy-free, egg-free, gluten-free, heart-healthy, high protein, low added sugars, low sodium, low calorie, nut-free, and soy-free

**Tips:**

Instead of freezing half, you can bake the full recipe in a 9 x 13-inch baking pan. In Step 6, bake, covered, for an additional 10 minutes.

To keep for later: Who doesn't enjoy having leftovers? This recipe prepares two meals: one for today and one to store for up to a month (see Step 5).

To prepare from frozen, thaw overnight in the refrigerator before baking as stated in Steps 6–7, adding 10 minutes of baking time once uncovered.

## No. 12: Sweet Potato and Black Bean Burgers

For those of us who miss having a burger now and then, this recipe will help you overcome those cravings. It is a vegan sweet potato and black bean burger spiced with curry powder that is easy to make.

I love that using your hands gives you a soft, uniform texture, while the outside gets crispy by cooking in a cast iron pan. For those who are allergic to gluten, substitute the bun for a lettuce wrap and use gluten-free oats.

**Preparation Time:** 15 Minutes

**Additional Time:** 30 Minutes

**Overall Time:** 45 Minutes

**Portions:** 4

**Produced:** 4 Burgers

**Ingredients:**

- 2 cups sweet potato grated
- 1/2 cup rolled oats, old-fashioned
- 1 cup drained black beans with no salt added
- 1/2 cup scallions, chopped
- 1/4 cup mayonnaise (vegan)
- 1 tablespoon of tomato paste (no salt added)
- 1 teaspoon of curry powder
- 1/8 teaspoon of salt
- 1/2 cup unsweetened plain almond milk yogurt
- 2 tablespoons of fresh dill chopped
- 2 tablespoons of lemon juice
- 2 tablespoons of extra-virgin olive oil
- 4 toasted whole wheat hamburger buns
- 1 cup cucumber, thinly sliced

**Directions:**

1. Squeeze grated sweet potato to remove extra moisture; place in a large mixing bowl.
2. In a food processor, pulse the oats until finely ground; add to the bowl containing the sweet potatoes.
3. Mash together the beans, scallions, mayonnaise, tomato paste, curry powder, and salt in a mixing bowl.
4. Form into four 1/2-inch-thick patties.
5. Refrigerate the patties for 30 minutes on a platter.
6. In a small bowl, combine the yogurt, dill, and lemon juice; set aside.
7. In a large cast-iron skillet, heat the oil over medium-high heat.
8. Cook until the patties are golden brown, about 3 minutes per side.
9. Distribute the yogurt sauce equally between the top and bottom bun

halves.

10. Replace the top bun halves and top each bottom bun half with a burger and cucumber slices. Eat Up!

**Nutritional Information:** (Per Serving)

454 Calories

22 grams of fat

54 grams of carbs

12 grams of protein

**Nutritional Profile:**

Diabetes-appropriate, bone health, dairy-free, egg-free, healthy aging, heart health, high calcium, high fiber, low sodium, vegan, vegetarian

**Tips:**

Plan when making this dish: prepare patties (Step 1), wrap them, and refrigerate them for up to 2 days.

**No. 13: Pork and Green Chile Stew**

This hearty stew recipe is packed with potatoes, hominy, green chiles, and pork sirloin chunks. I enjoy stews, and this recipe is so simple; just throw it in your slow cooker in the morning and forget about it until you get home for dinner; it only takes 25 minutes to prepare.

**Preparation Time:** 25 Minutes

**Additional Time:** 4 Hours

**Overall Time:** 4 Hours, 25 Minutes

**Portions:** 6 People

**Produced:** 6 Servings

**Ingredients:**

- 2 pounds of boneless pork sirloin or shoulder roast
- 1 tablespoon of vegetable oil
- 1/2 cup finely sliced onion (1 medium)
- 4 cups of peeled and diced medium potatoes
- 3 cups of water
- 1 (15-ounce) can of drained hominy or whole kernel corn 2 (4-ounce) cans of diced green chile peppers
- 2 tablespoons of tapioca (quick-cooking)
- 1 teaspoon of garlic salt
- 1/2 teaspoon cumin powder
- 1/2 teaspoon of ancho chile powder
- 1/2 teaspoon black pepper
- 1/4 teaspoon crushed dried oregano
- 1 tablespoon fresh cilantro, chopped

**Equipment:** 3 ½ to 4 ½ quart slow cooker

**Directions:**

1. Remove the fat from the meat. Cut the meat into 1/2-inch chunks.
2. In a large skillet, cook half of the meat in heated oil over medium-high heat.
3. Remove the meat from the skillet using a slotted spoon.
4. Repeat with the rest of the meat and onion.
5. Drain the grease and place the meat and onion in a 3-1/2 to 4-1/2-quart slow cooker.
6. Add the potatoes, water, hominy, green chile peppers, tapioca, garlic salt, cumin, ancho chile powder, ground pepper, and oregano, and mix well.
7. Cook on low for 7 to 8 hours or on high for 4 to 5 hours, covered.

8. Garnish each plate with cilantro, if desired.

**Nutritional Information:** (Per Serving)
180 Calories
4 grams of fat
23 grams of carbs
15 grams of protein

**Nutritional Profile:**
Diabetes-appropriate, heart-healthy, low-calorie, dairy-free, egg-free, gluten-free, low-sodium, nut-free, high blood pressure-free, and soy-free

## No. 14: Maple-Roasted Chicken Thighs with Sweet Potato Wedges and Brussels Sprouts

One of my favorite seasons is fall, and this recipe brings a lot of my seasonal favorites together in a very simple recipe using just a sheet pan.

**Preparation Time:** 20 Minutes

**Additional Time:** 30 Minutes

**Overall Time:** 50 Minutes

**Portions:** 4

**Produced:** 4 Servings

**Ingredients:**

- 2 tablespoons of pure maple syrup
- 4 teaspoons of olive oil
- 1 tablespoon of fresh thyme clipped

- 1/2 teaspoon of salt
- 1/2 teaspoon of black pepper
- 1 pound peeled and cut into 1-inch slices of sweet potatoes
- 1 pound of trimmed and halved Brussels sprouts
- Nonstick cooking spray
- 4 skinned, bone-in chicken thighs
- 3 tablespoons of dried cranberries, snipped
- 3 tablespoons of chopped toasted pecans

**Directions:**

1. Preheat the oven to 425 degrees Fahrenheit.
2. Combine maple syrup, 1 teaspoon oil, thyme, 1/4 teaspoon salt, and 1/4 teaspoon pepper in a small bowl.
3. Combine sweet potatoes and Brussels sprouts in a large mixing dish.
4. Drizzle with the remaining 1 tablespoon oil and season with the remaining 1/4 teaspoon salt and 1/4 teaspoon pepper; toss to coat.
5. Wrap foil around a 15-by-10-inch baking pan. After 5 minutes in the oven, heat the prepared pan.
6. Spray the pan with cooking spray after it has been removed from the oven.
7. Place the chicken in the center of the pan, meaty sides down.
8. Roast the vegetables around the chicken for 15 minutes.
9. Brush the maple syrup mixture over the chicken and vegetables.
10. Roast for another 15 minutes, or until the chicken is cooked through (at least 175 degrees Fahrenheit) and the potatoes are soft.
11. Serve with pecans and cranberries on top. Enjoy!

**Nutritional Information:** (Per Serving)
436 Calories
14 grams of fat
45 grams of carbs
34 grams of protein

**Nutritional Profile:**

Diabetes-appropriate, dairy-free, egg-free, gluten-free, healthy again, healthy immunity, healthy pregnancy, heart-healthy, high blood pressure, high fiber, high protein, low sodium, low calorie, soy-free

**No. 15: Skillet Chicken Pot Pie**

As a kid, I ate a lot of pot pies. So finding a recipe that uses a store-bought pie crust, frozen vegetables, and precooked chicken makes preparing this pot pie a breeze. This healthy dinner meal takes me back to some of the best comfort food I've ever had.

**Preparation Time:** 35 Minutes

**Additional Time:** 25 Minutes

**Overall Time:** 1 hour

**Portions:** 6 People

**Produced:** 1 Pot pie

**Ingredients:**

- 1-1/2 cups low-sodium chicken broth
- 2 tablespoons of all-purpose flour
- 1 tablespoon of olive oil
- 1 package (8 oz.) sliced cremini mushrooms
- 1 cup finely chopped onion
- 6 minced garlic cloves
- 1/2 cup frozen carrots and peas (7 oz.)
- 1 tablespoon fresh sage, chopped
- 1 tablespoon fresh thyme leaves, plus garnish sprigs

- 1/2 teaspoon of salt
- 1/2 teaspoon black pepper
- 1 pound cooked shredded chicken (approximately 3 cups; see tips below)
- 1 premade pie crust (7 to 8 ounces), thawed if frozen
- 1 lightly beaten egg white

**Equipment:** 10-inch cast iron skillet or oven-safe nonstick skillet

**Directions:**

1. Preheat the oven to 425 degrees Fahrenheit.
2. In a medium mixing bowl, combine 1/4 cup broth and flour; set aside.
3. Over medium-high heat, heat the oil in a 10-inch cast iron skillet or oven-safe nonstick skillet.
4. Cook until the mushrooms are browned, 6 to 8 minutes. Turn the heat down to medium.
5. Cook until the onion and garlic are soft, 4 to 6 minutes.
6. Scrape off any browned parts before adding the remaining 1/4 cup of broth.
7. Combine the leftover broth flour mixture, peas and carrots, sage, thyme, salt, and pepper in a large mixing bowl.
8. Bring to a boil while constantly stirring.
9. Cook, stirring occasionally, for about 10 minutes, or until the vegetables are soft.
10. Remove from the heat and mix in the chicken.
11. Fold the edges of the pie dough over the chicken mixture as needed.
12. To let steam escape, make four 4-inch slits in the crust. Brush with beaten egg white.
13. Bake for 20 to 25 minutes, or until the crust is brown and the filling is bubbling.
14. Allow 10 minutes to cool before serving.
15. If preferred, garnish with thyme sprigs.

**Nutritional Information:** (Per Serving)

336 Calories

13 grams of fat

26 grams of carbs

29 grams of protein

**Nutritional Profile:**

Diabetes-appropriate, dairy-free, egg-free, healthy again, healthy immunity, heart-healthy, high protein, low sodium, low calorie, nut-free, and soy-free

**Tips:**

To poach chicken, place 4 small boneless, skinless chicken thighs or 2 small boneless, skinless chicken breasts (12 ounces total) in a medium saucepan; cover with cold water. Bring to a boil over medium-high heat. Reduce heat to low, partially cover, and cook until an instant-read thermometer inserted in the thickest part registers 165 degrees Fahrenheit, 12 to 15 minutes. Transfer to a plate and shred into small pieces. Reserve the broth for use in another recipe; it will keep in the fridge for up to 4 days or in the freezer for up to 3 months.

**No. 16: Ginger Beef Stir Fry with Peppers**

If you, like me, enjoy a bit of extra heat in your meals, this dinner recipe is for you. Alternatively, you can alter the amount of chile-garlic sauce to suit your level of heat. Use the flat edge of a chef's knife or the flat bottom of a strong mug to smash the ginger. If desired, serve with whole-grain rice.

**Cook Time:** 30 Minutes

**Overall Time:** 30 Minutes

**Portions:** 4 People

**Ingredients:**

- 12 ounces of trimmed lean flank steak
- 1-1/2 teaspoons of cornstarch
- 1 tablespoon soy sauce (reduced sodium)
- 1 teaspoon of dry sherry plus 1 tablespoon
- 1 teaspoon of vegetable oil plus 1 tablespoon
- 4 teaspoons of hoisin sauce
- 4 teaspoons of ketchup
- 1 to 3 teaspoons of Sriracha or chili garlic sauce
- 3 peeled ginger slices, smashed, 1 small yellow onion, finely sliced
- 1 cup (1 inch) chopped green bell pepper
- 1 cup (1 inch) chopped red bell pepper
- 2 tablespoons of unsalted beef broth

**Equipment:** a 14-inch flat-bottomed carbon steel wok or a 12-inch stainless steel skillet

**Directions:**

1. Cut the beef into 2-inch-wide strips against the grain.
2. Cut each strip into 14-inch-thick pieces against the grain.
3. In a medium mixing bowl, combine the meat, cornstarch, 1-1/2 teaspoons soy sauce, and 1 teaspoon sherry; stir until the cornstarch is no longer visible.
4. Stir in 1 teaspoon of oil until the beef is lightly covered.
5. In a separate bowl, combine hoisin sauce, ketchup, chili garlic sauce (or Sriracha) to taste, then the remaining 1-1/2 tsp soy sauce and 1 tbsp sherry. Set aside.
6. Over high heat, heat a 14-inch flat-bottomed carbon steel wok (or a 12-inch stainless steel skillet) until a drop of water vaporizes within 1 to 2 seconds of contact.
7. Swirl in the remaining 1 tablespoon of oil.

8. Stir in the ginger for about 10 seconds, or until aromatic. Push the ginger to the pan's sides and top with the beef in an equal layer.

9. Cook, stirring occasionally, until the beef begins to brown, about 1 minute.

10. Stir in the onion for 30 seconds to 1 minute more, or until the beef is lightly browned but not cooked through.

11. Put the steak and onion combination on a plate.

12. Add the green and red peppers, as well as the broth, to the pan.

13. Cook, covered, over high heat for 1 minute, or until the peppers are brilliant green and red and almost all of the liquid has been absorbed.

14. Return the steak, onion, and any liquids to the pan.

15. Stir-fry for 30 seconds to 1 minute, or until the meat is just cooked through and the peppers are soft and crunchy.

16. If preferred, remove the ginger.

**Nutritional Information:** (Per Serving)

215 Calories

10 grams of fat

11 grams of carbs

20 grams of protein

**Nutritional Profile:**

Diabetes-appropriate, low-carbohydrate

**No. 17: Jambalaya Stuffed Peppers**

Just thinking about this dish makes me hungry. This nutritious recipe uses a pepper that has been stuffed with a tasty jambalaya filling of chicken and Cajun seasonings and baked inside a bell pepper. Traditional jambalaya is cooked using green bell peppers, but you can substitute green, yellow, or orange peppers (or a combination) for this recipe. Look for bell peppers with even bottoms so they can stand upright on their own.

**Preparation Time:** 40 Minutes

**Additional Time:** 30 Minutes

**Overall Time:** 1 Hour, 10 Minutes

**Portions:** 6 People

**Produced:** 6 Peppers

**Ingredients:**

- 6 huge bell peppers, green, yellow, or orange (your choice)
- 1-1/2 pound boneless, skinless chicken thighs, trimmed and cut into 1-inch chunks
- 2 tablespoons of salt-free olive oil and split Cajun seasoning (see tips below)
- 2 tablespoons of olive oil, 1 link andouille sausage (3–4 ounces), 1/2 cup diced celery
- 1/2 cup diced tiny onion
- 1/2 teaspoon salt 2 minced garlic cloves
- 1 can of diced tomatoes (14 oz.)
- 1/4 cup tomato paste
- 1 cup chicken broth (low sodium)
- 1 cup instant brown rice, uncooked

**Directions:**

1. Preheat the oven to 400 degrees Fahrenheit.
2. Using parchment paper or foil, line a large, rimmed baking sheet.
3. Remove the pepper tops and carefully remove the core and seeds, being careful not to fracture the skin.
4. Set aside the pepper tops to dice.

5. Bake the peppers for 20 minutes on the prepared baking sheet.

6. Remove from oven and set aside to cool; remove any liquid that has gathered in the bottom of the peppers.

7. Meanwhile, season the chicken with 1 tablespoon of Cajun seasoning on all sides. In a large skillet over medium heat, heat 1 tablespoon of oil.

8. Cook for 4 to 6 minutes, turning to brown on all sides, using half of the chicken.

9. With a slotted spoon, transfer the chicken to a medium bowl. Repeat with the remaining 1 tablespoon of olive oil and chicken.

10. Cook, tossing periodically, until the sausage is gently browned, 1 to 2 minutes in the now-empty skillet.

11. Cook, stirring frequently, until the celery, onion, and saved chopped pepper are translucent, 3 to 5 minutes.

12. Cook, stirring constantly, for 30 seconds after adding garlic, the remaining 1 tablespoon Cajun seasoning, and salt.

13. Stir in the tomatoes and tomato paste, scraping off any brown pieces from the bottom of the pan.

14. Stir in the broth, rice, and chicken with any accumulated juices.

15. Bring the water to a boil. Reduce the heat to maintain a simmer and cook, stirring periodically, for 5 to 10 minutes, or until the chicken is cooked through and the rice is mushy.

16. Remove the pan from the heat and continue to stir.

17. Allow to stand, covered, for 10 minutes or until all of the liquid has been absorbed.

18. Divide the chicken mixture evenly among the peppers, spooning approximately 1-1/4 cups into each and mounding it on top if required.

19. Bake for 20 minutes, or until thoroughly heated.

**Nutritional Information:** (Per Serving)

346 Calories

12 grams of fat

30 grams of carbs

31 grams of protein

**Nutritional Profile:**

Diabetes-appropriate, dairy-free, egg-free, gluten-free, healthy aging, healthy immunity, heart-healthy, high protein, low added sugars, low sodium, low calorie, nut-free, and soy-free

**Tips:**

If you prefer homemade Cajun seasoning because it has more flavor and fewer preservatives than the store-bought versions, For salt-free Cajun seasoning, mix 1 Tbsp. paprika, 1 tsp. each onion powder and garlic powder, ½ tsp. each dried oregano and thyme, and ¼ tsp. each cayenne and ground pepper. You will have slightly more than you need for this recipe; use it to season eggs, chicken, fish, or vegetables. Want to have extra on hand? Multiply these amounts by four. Store in a covered jar for up to 6 months.

**No. 18: Charred Shrimp, Pesto, and Quinoa Bowls**

These shrimp, pesto, and quinoa bowls are so delicious, healthy for diabetics, easy to cook, and take less than 30 minutes to prep. This is the ultimate easy weeknight dinner. Alternatively, you can add additional vegetables and swap the shrimp for chicken, steak, tofu, or edamame, if desired.

**Preparation Time:** 25 Minutes

**Overall Time:** 25 Minutes

**Portions:** 4

**Produced:** 10 Cups

**Ingredients:**

- 1/3 cup pesto (prepared)

- 2 tablespoons of balsamic vinegar
- 1 tablespoon of olive oil (extra virgin)
- 1/2 teaspoon salt, 1/4 teaspoon black pepper
- 1 pound of large peeled and deveined shrimp (16–20 counts), patted dry
- Arugula, 4 cups
- 2 cups quinoa, cooked
- 1 cup cherry tomatoes, halved
- 1 diced avocado

**Directions:**

1. Combine the pesto, vinegar, oil, salt, and pepper in a large mixing bowl.
2. 4 tablespoons of the mixture should be transferred to a small bowl; set both bowls aside.
3. Melt the butter in a large cast-iron skillet over medium-high heat.
4. Cook, tossing constantly, until the shrimp are just cooked through with a faint sear, 4 to 5 minutes. Transfer to a plate.
5. Toss the arugula and quinoa with the vinaigrette in a large mixing bowl. Divide the arugula mixture among four serving dishes.
6. Serve with tomatoes, avocado, and shrimp on top.
7. Drizzle 1 tablespoon of the leftover pesto mixture over each bowl.

**Nutritional Information:** (Per Serving)
429 Calories
22 grams of fat
29 grams of carbs
31 grams of protein

**Nutritional Profile:**
Diabetes-appropriate, bone health, egg-free, gluten-free, healthy aging, healthy immunity, heart-healthy, high protein, low sodium, low calorie, soy-free

**Tips:**

To prepare ahead of time: Cover and refrigerate the dressing (Step 1) for up to 2 days.

**No. 19: Cilantro Bean Burgers with Creamy Avocado Lime Slaw**

Bean patties themselves have less saturated fat and more fiber than regular beef patties. They are also much cheaper and easier to cook indoors, and I promise they are just as satisfying, especially with the mouthwatering creamy slaw on top. Enjoy!

**Preparation Time:** 45 Minutes

**Overall Time:** 45 Minutes

**Portions:** 4

**Produced:** 4 Servings

**Ingredients:**

- 1 (15-ounce) can of drained black beans, no salt added
- 2 minced and split garlic cloves
- 1/2 teaspoon cumin, 1/2 teaspoon salt, divided
- 1/8 teaspoon of ground pepper
- 1/4 cup tortilla chips or panko breadcrumbs
- 1/4 cup quick-cook oats
- 2 tablespoons of chopped toasted pumpkin seeds
- 1/2 cup divided plus 2 tablespoons of chopped fresh cilantro
- 1 big, lightly beaten egg
- 1/4 cup plain, low-fat Greek yogurt
- 1/2 avocado

- 2 tablespoons of lime juice 1 teaspoon of lime zest
- 2 tablespoons of water
- 4 cups shredded (green and/or red) cabbage
- 2 teaspoons of olive oil
- 4 halved and toasted whole wheat buns

## Directions:

1. In a medium mixing bowl, combine the beans, half of the garlic, cumin, 1/4 teaspoon salt, and pepper.
2. Mash the beans with a fork until they are fully mashed.
3. Combine crushed chips (or panko), oats, pumpkin seeds, 2 tablespoons of cilantro, and an egg in a mixing bowl.
4. Divide the ingredients into four equal halves and form patties.
5. Refrigerate for 30 minutes before cooking on a platter.
6. Meanwhile, in a blender or food processor, combine the remaining 1/2 cup cilantro, remaining garlic, yogurt, avocado, lime juice, and water. Blend until smooth.
7. Transfer to a large mixing bowl. Stir in the lime zest and 1/4 teaspoon salt.
8. Toss in the cabbage to mix.
9. In a large nonstick skillet over medium-high heat, heat the oil.
10. Cook for 6 minutes after adding the burgers.
11. Turn them over, decrease the heat to medium, cover, and cook for 5 to 6 minutes more, or until golden brown and warmed through.
12. Serve the burgers on buns with 1/4 cup of cabbage slaw on top. Serve the leftover slaw on the side.

## Nutritional Information: (Per Serving)
368 Calories
11 grams of fat
55 grams of carbs
16 grams of protein

**Nutritional Profile:**

Diabetes-appropriate, high fiber, high protein, healthy aging, low calorie, nut-free, soy-free, vegetarian

**No. 20: Slow Cooker Chicken and White Bean Stew**

For those busy weeknight dinners, this load-and-go slow cooker chicken recipe is perfect! Serve this Tuscan-inspired dish with crusty bread, a glass of Chianti, and a salad if desired.

**Preparation Time:** 15 Minutes

**Additional Time:** 7 Hours, 20 Minutes

**Overall Time:** 7 Hours, 35 Minutes

**Portions:** 6

**Produced:** 7 ½ Cups

**Ingredients:**

- 1 pound of dried cannellini beans, soaked and drained overnight (see tips below).
- 6 cups chicken broth, unsalted
- 1 cup yellow onion, chopped
- 1 cup carrots, sliced
- 1 teaspoon fresh rosemary, coarsely chopped
- 1 (4 ounces) Parmesan cheese rind plus 2/3 cup shredded Parmesan, split
- 4 cups kale, chopped
- 1 tablespoon of lemon juice
- 1/2 teaspoon kosher salt
- 1/2 teaspoon black pepper

- 2 tablespoons of extra-virgin olive oil
- 1/4 cup parsley leaves, flat-leaf

**Directions:**

1. In a 6-quart slow cooker, combine the beans, broth, onion, carrots, rosemary, and Parmesan rind. Serve with chicken on top.
2. Cook on low for 7 to 8 hours, or until the beans and veggies are cooked.
3. Transfer the chicken to a clean cutting board and set aside for 10 minutes, or until cool enough to handle.
4. Remove the bones from the chicken and shred it.
5. Stir in the kale and return the chicken to the slow cooker.
6. Cook, covered, on high for 20 to 30 minutes, or until the kale is soft.
7. Remove the Parmesan rind and stir in the lemon juice, salt, and pepper.
8. Drizzle the stew with oil and top with Parmesan and parsley.

**Nutritional Information:** (Per Serving)
493 Calories
11 grams of fat
54 grams of carbs
44 grams of protein

**Nutritional Profile:**
Diabetes-appropriate, heart-healthy, healthy aging, healthy immunity, high blood pressure, high fiber, low added sugars, low sodium, and low calories

**Tips:**

To save time, you can substitute 4 (15-ounce) cans of rinsed cannellini beans for the soaked dried beans.

**No. 21: Sheet Pan Salmon with Sweet Potatoes and Broccoli**

The healthy, vibrant combo of cheese, cilantro, chili, and lime inspired by Mexican street corn makes this salmon sheet pan dinner bursting with flavor.

**Preparation Time:** 30 Minutes

**Additional Time:** 15 Minutes

**Overall Time:** 45 Minutes

**Portions:** 4

**Produced:** 4 Servings

**Ingredients:**

- 3 tablespoons of light mayonnaise
- 1 teaspoon of chili powder
- 2 medium peeled and cut into 1-inch cubes sweet potatoes
- 4 teaspoons of olive oil, 1/2 teaspoon salt, and 1/4 teaspoon ground pepper
- 8 ounces of broccoli florets (1 medium crown)
- 14 pounds of salmon fillet, divided into four parts
- 2 limes, zest 1 lime, juice, and serve in wedges.
- 1/4 cup crumbled feta or cotija
- 1/2 cup fresh cilantro, chopped

**Directions:**

1. Preheat the oven to 425 degrees Fahrenheit. Coat a large, rimmed baking sheet with foil and cooking spray.
2. In a small bowl, combine mayonnaise and chili powder. Place aside.
3. In a medium mixing bowl, combine sweet potatoes, 2 teaspoons oil, 1/4 teaspoon salt, and 1/8 teaspoon pepper.

174

4. Spread the mixture on the prepared baking sheet. 15 minutes in the oven

5. Meanwhile, in the same bowl, combine the broccoli with the remaining 2 tablespoons of oil, 1/4 teaspoon salt, and 1/8 teaspoon of pepper.

6. Take the baking sheet out of the oven. Stir the sweet potatoes and push them to the pan's sides.

7. Place the salmon in the center of the pan, then the broccoli on either side.

8. 2 tablespoons of the mayonnaise mixture should be spread over the salmon.

9. Bake for 15 minutes, or until the sweet potatoes are soft and the salmon flakes easily with a fork.

10. Meanwhile, combine the remaining 1 tablespoon of mayonnaise with the lime zest and juice.

11. Serve the salmon on four dishes, topped with cheese and cilantro.

12. Drizzle the lime mayonnaise sauce over the sweet potatoes and broccoli on each plate.

13. Serve with the remaining sauce and lime wedges.

**Nutritional Information:** (Per Serving)
504 Calories
26 grams of fat
34 grams of carbs
34 grams of protein

**Nutritional Profile:**
Diabetes-appropriate, healthy aging, high protein, gluten-free, nut-free, soy-free, omega-3

**No. 22: Lemon Chicken Pasta**

I enjoy the combination of lemon zest and toasted breadcrumbs in this lemon chicken pasta recipe. For a healthy dinner that is excellent for diabetics, use rotisserie chicken, quick-cooking spiralized zucchini, and baby zucchini to make a whole meal in about 10 minutes!

**Preparation Time:** 10 Minutes

**Overall Time:** 10 Minutes

**Portions:** 1

**Produced:** 2 Cups

**Ingredients:**

- 2 teaspoons of extra-virgin olive oil
- 1 cup spiralized zucchini (see tips below)
- 1 cup of fresh baby spinach
- 1/2 cup skinless shredded rotisserie chicken breast
- 1/8 teaspoon salt
- 1/8 teaspoon black pepper
- 1/2 cup cooked wholegrain spaghetti
- 2 tablespoons of Parmesan cheese, grated
- 1 tablespoon of fresh lemon juice 1 teaspoon grated lemon zest
- 1 tablespoon toasted panko breadcrumbs (see tips below)

**Directions:**

1. In a large nonstick skillet over medium heat, heat the oil.
2. Cook for 1 minute after adding the zucchini.
3. Cook for 1 minute more after adding the spinach and chicken.
4. Remove from the heat and season with salt and pepper.
5. Toss in the cooked spaghetti, Parmesan, lemon zest, and lemon juice.
6. Serve topped with toasted panko.

**Equipment:** Vegetable spiralizer

**Nutritional Information:** (Per Serving)
350 Calories
15 grams of fat
27 grams of carbs
29 grams of protein

**Nutritional Profile:**
Diabetes-appropriate, healthy aging, healthy immunity, high protein, low added sugars, low calories, egg-free, nut-free, and soy-free

**Tips:**

Make your zucchini noodles with a spiralizer; you'll need 1 small zucchini (about 2 ounces) for 1 cup of zoodles. Or look for a package of fresh zucchini noodles in the produce department.

To toast panko breadcrumbs, set a small skillet over medium heat. Add panko and cook, stirring often, until golden, about 2 minutes. For extra flavor, melt 1 tsp. butter in the pan before toasting the breadcrumbs. Note that you can do this step first, using the same pan you'll use to prepare the rest of the recipe.

To save it for later, cook the pasta ahead of time and chill it.

**No. 23: Roasted Root Veggies and Greens Over Spiced Lentils**

For those leftover roasted root veggies in your fridge, top them with an earthy bowl of lentils for an easy weeknight dinner. Keep it vegan or add a drizzle of plain yogurt for extra richness if desired.

**Preparation Time:** 20 Minutes

**Additional Time:** 25 Minutes

**Overall Time:** 45 Minutes

**Portions:** 2

**Produced:** 2 Servings

**Ingredients:**

## Lentils

- 1-1/2 cup water
- 1/2 cup black beluga lentils or French green lentils (see tips below)
- 1 tsp. garlic powder
- 1/2 teaspoon coriander powder
- 1/2 teaspoon cumin powder
- 1/4 teaspoon allspice powder
- 1/4 teaspoon of kosher salt
- 1/8 teaspoon sumac, optional
- 2 tablespoons of lemon juice
- 1 teaspoon extra virgin olive oil

## Vegetables

- 1 tablespoon olive oil (extra virgin)
- 1 garlic clove, mashed
- 1/2 cup roasted root veggies
- 2 cups kale or beet greens, chopped
- 1 teaspoon of coriander powder
- 1/8 teaspoon black pepper
- Kosher salt, a pinch
- 2 tablespoons of tahini or plain low-fat yogurt

- Garnish with fresh parsley.

## Directions:

1. In a medium pot, add water, lentils, garlic powder, 1/2 teaspoon each of coriander, cumin, allspice, 1/4 teaspoon each of salt, and sumac (if using).
2. Bring the water to a boil. Reduce the heat to maintain a simmer, cover, and cook until the vegetables are soft, 25 to 30 minutes.
3. Uncover and continue to boil for another 5 minutes, or until the liquid has slightly reduced.
4. Drain. Mix in 1 teaspoon of oil and lemon juice.
5. Meanwhile, heat oil in a large skillet over medium heat to prepare the vegetables.
6. Cook until the garlic is aromatic, about 1 to 2 minutes.
7. Cook, stirring frequently, until the roasted root vegetables are cooked through, 2 to 4 minutes.
8. Cook until the kale (or beet greens) is barely wilted, 2 to 3 minutes.
9. Combine the coriander, pepper, and salt in a mixing bowl.
10. Serve the vegetables with tahini (or yogurt) on top of the lentils.
11. If desired, garnish with parsley.

## Nutritional Information: (Per Serving)

453 Calories

22 grams of fat

50 grams of carbs

18 grams of protein

## Nutritional Profile:

Diabetes-appropriate, dairy-free, egg-free, gluten-free, healthy aging, healthy immunity, healthy pregnancy, heart-healthy, high fiber, high protein, low sodium, low calorie, nut-free, soy-free, vegan, vegetarian

**Tips:**

I like black beluga lentils or French green lentils instead of brown when I want lentils that hold their shape instead of breaking down when cooked. Look for them in natural food stores and some supermarkets.

**No. 24: Kung Pao Chicken with Bell Peppers**

This is a wonderfully simple chicken recipe that you should add to your dinner repertoire. In this stir-fry, a brief marinade tenderizes the chicken and adds flavor. A little oil toward the end of the marinade coats the chicken and keeps it from sticking to the pan.

**Preparation Time:** 30 Minutes

**Overall Time:** 30 Minutes

**Portions:** 4

**Produced:** 4 Cups

**Ingredients:**

- 1 pound boneless, skinless chicken breast, sliced 1/4 inch thick
- 2 teaspoons of reduced-sodium soy sauce plus 1 tablespoon
- 1 teaspoon of dry sherry plus 1 tablespoon
- 2 teaspoons of cornstarch
- 2 teaspoons of sesame oil, roasted
- 2 tablespoons of unseasoned chicken broth
- 2 tablespoons of balsamic vinegar
- 2 teaspoons of. chili-garlic sauce (see tips below)
- 2 tablespoons vegetable oil (divided)
- 3 fresh ginger slices, peeled and smashed (see recommendations below)

- 1 medium red bell pepper, peeled and sliced into 1-inch squares
- 1 medium green bell pepper, peeled and sliced into 1-inch squares
- 1/4 teaspoon salt
- 2 tablespoons of dry-roasted unsalted peanuts

**Directions:**

1. In a medium mixing bowl, combine the chicken, 2 tablespoons soy sauce, 1 teaspoon sherry, and cornstarch.
2. Stir until the cornstarch is completely dissolved.
3. Stir in the sesame oil until the chicken is lightly covered.
4. In a small bowl, combine broth, vinegar, chile-garlic garlic sauce, the remaining 1 tablespoon soy sauce, and 1 tablespoon sherry. Set aside.
5. Over high heat, heat a 14-inch flat-bottomed carbon steel wok or a 12-inch stainless steel skillet until a drop of water vaporizes within 1 to 2 seconds of contact.
6. Swirl in 1 tablespoon of vegetable oil.
7. Stir in the ginger for about 10 seconds, or until aromatic.
8. Push the ginger slices to the sides of the pan and top with the chicken in an equal layer.
9. Cook, stirring occasionally, until it begins to brown, about 1 minute.
10. Stir-fry the chicken for 1 minute more, until lightly browned but not cooked through, using a metal spatula. Place on a platter.
11. Stir in the remaining 1 tablespoon of vegetable oil.
12. Stir in the bell peppers for 1 minute.
13. Return the chicken to the pan with the saved sauce, season with salt, and stir fry for 1 to 3 minutes, or until the chicken is cooked through.
14. Remove from the heat and top with the peanuts.

**Equipment:** 14-inch flat-bottomed carbon steel wok or 12-inch stainless steel skillet

**Nutritional Information:** (Per Serving)

264 Calories

14 grams of fat

7 grams of carbs

25 grams of protein

**Nutritional Profile:**

Diabetes-appropriate, dairy-free, egg-free, healthy aging, healthy immunity, high protein, low carbohydrate, low calorie

**Tips:**

You can find chile-garlic sauce in the Asian food aisle of most major grocery stores. It is a red sauce often sold in a clear plastic jar. If you can't find it, you can add ½ tsp. crushed red pepper and 1 tsp. minced garlic with ginger in Step 3. A slice of ginger is about the size of a quarter. You can smash it with the side of a chef's knife or with the bottom of a small pot or pan.

**No. 25: Four Bean and Pumpkin Chili**

This diabetic-friendly, healthy vegetarian chili dish has a fragrant touch of cinnamon for added flavor. Alternatively, you can top your dinner with whatever suits your taste.

**Preparation Time:** 45 Minutes

**Additional Time:** 40 Minutes

**Overall Time:** 1 Hour, 25 Minutes

**Portions:** 8

**Produced:** 8 servings

## Ingredients:

- 1 tablespoon of olive oil (extra virgin)
- 3 cups finely chopped onion
- 1-1/2 cup carrot, chopped
- 3 large garlic cloves, minced
- 4 cups vegetable broth (low sodium)
- 3 cups chopped butternut squash or pumpkin
- 1 can of crushed tomatoes (28 oz.) No salt added.
- 4 (15-ounce) cans of rinsed low-sodium beans (black, great northern, pinto, and/or red)
- 3 tablespoons of chili powder
- 2 teaspoons of cumin powder
- 1 teaspoon of cinnamon powder
- 3/4 teaspoon salt
- 1/4 teaspoon cayenne pepper, or more to taste
- Garnish with diced onion, sliced jalapenos, Cotija cheese, and/or pepitas.

## Directions:

1. In a big pot, heat the oil over medium-high heat.
2. Cook, stirring frequently, until the onion begins to brown, about 5 minutes.
3. Reduce the heat to medium, add the carrot, and simmer, stirring frequently, until the veggies are tender, 4 to 5 minutes more.
4. Cook, stirring constantly, for 1 minute.
5. Bring the broth to a boil over high heat, scraping off any browned bits.
6. Combine the pumpkin (or squash), tomatoes, beans, chili powder, cumin, cinnamon, salt, and cayenne pepper (if using).
7. Return to a boil, covered. Reduce the heat to maintain a slow simmer and cook, uncovered, for 30 minutes, or until the pumpkin (or squash) is soft.
8. If desired, garnish with onion, jalapenos, cheese, and/or pepitas.

**Nutritional Information:** (Per Serving)

276 Calories

3 grams of fat

49 grams of carbs

14 grams of protein

**Nutritional Profile:**

Diabetes-appropriate, dairy-free, egg-free, heart-healthy, healthy aging, healthy immunity, high fiber, high blood pressure, low calorie, low sodium, nut-free, soy-free, vegan, vegetarian

**Tips:**

Serve garnished with onion, jalapenos, cheese, and/or pepitas, if desired.

## No. 26: Garlic Roasted Salmon and Brussels Sprouts

For a very simple evening dinner, roast salmon on top of Brussels sprouts and garlic and flavor it with wine and fresh oregano. It is a sophisticated meal that you can serve when company is over. Serve with wholewheat couscous if desired.

**Cook Time:** 25 Minutes

**Additional Time:** 20 Minutes

**Overall Time:** 45 Minutes

**Portions:** 6

**Produced:** 6 Servings

**Ingredients:**

- 14 huge garlic cloves, divided into 1/4 cup extra virgin olive oil
- 2 tablespoons finely chopped fresh oregano, 1 teaspoon salt, 3/4 teaspoon freshly ground pepper, and 6 cups trimmed and sliced Brussels sprouts 3/4 cup white wine, ideally Chardonnay
- 2 pounds peeled and sliced into 6 parts wild-caught salmon fillet
- Slices of lemon

## Directions:

1. Preheat the oven to 450 degrees Fahrenheit.
2. In a small bowl, blend 2 garlic cloves, 1 tablespoon oregano, 1/2 teaspoon salt, and 1/4 teaspoon pepper.
3. In a large roasting pan, combine the remaining garlic, Brussels sprouts, and 3 tablespoons of seasoned oil.
4. Roast for 15 minutes, stirring once.
5. Pour the remaining oil mixture over the wine.
6. Remove the skillet from the oven, toss in the vegetables, and top with the salmon.
7. Drizzle the wine mixture over the top.
8. Sprinkle with the remaining 1 tablespoon of oregano, as well as 1/2 teaspoon salt and pepper.
9. Bake for 5 to 10 minutes more, or until the salmon is just cooked through.
10. With lemon slices, serve.

## Nutritional Information: (Per Serving)

334 Calories

15 grams of fat

10 grams of carbs

33 grams of protein

## Nutritional Profile:

Diabetes-appropriate, dairy-free, gluten-free, bone health, healthy aging, healthy immunity, heart health, high blood pressure, high protein, low added sugars, low carbohydrate, low sodium, low calorie

## No. 27: Broccolini, Chicken Sausage, and Orzo Skillet

This simple skillet supper is perfect for those hectic evenings. In less than 30 minutes, the sausage and orzo simmer beautifully together in chicken stock, resulting in a creamy, risotto-like meal.

**Preparation Time:** 20 Minutes

**Additional Time:** 10 Minutes

**Overall Time:** 30 Minutes

**Portions:** 4

**Produced:** 4 Servings

**Ingredients:**

- 2 teaspoons of olive oil
- 6 ounces of cooked chicken sausage, sliced into 1/4-inch slices, such as Al Fresco Sweet Italian
- 1/2 cup finely chopped onion
- 1 cup orzo (whole wheat)
- 3 minced garlic cloves
- 1/4 teaspoon crushed red pepper, plus more for garnish 2-1/2 cups low-sodium chicken broth
- 1/4 teaspoon kosher salt
- 1 pound of trimmed broccolini or 4 cups of broccoli florets
- 1/4 cup grated Parmesan cheese plus more for garnish
- 2 teaspoons of lemon zest

## Directions:

1. Over medium-high heat, heat the oil in a 12-inch cast iron skillet or other large, heavy skillet.
2. Cook, tossing occasionally, until the sausage is browned, about 3 to 4 minutes.
3. Cook, stirring, for 1 minute more after adding orzo and garlic.
4. Combine broth, crushed red pepper, and salt in a mixing bowl.
5. Bring the water to a boil. Add broccolini (or broccoli).
6. Reduce the heat to low, cover, and cook until the orzo is soft, 8 to 10 minutes.
7. Cook, covered until the broth has been absorbed.
8. Combine the Parmesan and lemon zest in a mixing bowl.
9. If preferred, top with more Parmesan and crushed red pepper before serving.

## Nutritional Information: (Per Serving)

333 Calories

10 grams of fat

42 grams of carbs

18 grams of protein

## Nutritional Profile:

Diabetes-appropriate, nut-free, egg-free, high fiber, high protein, healthy aging, low calorie

## No. 28: Dan Dan Noodles with Shrimp

In just 30 minutes, these healthful and delicious dan dan noodles are blended with sesame soy sauce, shrimp, and peanuts. The preserved veggies from Sichuan offer a vibrant flash of acidic, slightly fermented flavor. If you want the most authentic flavor, look for them at an Asian grocery store, or substitute kimchi if preferred.

**Cook Time:** 30 Minutes

**Overall Time:** 30 Minutes

**Portions:** 6

**Produced:** 6 Servings

**Ingredients:**

- 12 oz. Chinese flat noodles (see tips below) or even linguine.
- 2 tablespoons of sugar
- 2 tablespoons of dark soy sauce (see tips below)
- 2 tablespoons of low-sodium soy sauce
- 2 tablespoons of Chinese sesame paste (see tips below) Alternatively, tahini
- 2 tablespoons of chili garlic sauce (see tips below)
- 2 tbsp. chicken broth (low sodium)
- 1 tbsp. cider vinegar
- 2 tbsp. Rinsed and sliced Sichuan preserved veggies or kimchi
- 2 tbsp. peanut or canola oil
- 16 medium raw shrimp (10 to 12 ounces). See tips below), peeled, and deveined
- 1/4 cup roasted, unsalted peanuts, diced
- 3 finely chopped scallions

**Directions:**

1. A large pot of water should be brought to a boil. Cook the noodles as directed on the packet.
2. Drain and rinse thoroughly. Pour into a large, shallow serving bowl.
3. Meanwhile, in a small bowl, add sugar, dark soy sauce, reduced-sodium soy sauce, sesame paste (or tahini), chile-garlic sauce, broth, and vinegar.

4. Place it close to the stove. Using a paper towel, pat dry the preserved veggies (or kimchi). Place it close to the stove.
5. Over medium-high heat, heat a 14-inch flat-bottom carbon steel wok or large cast iron pan.
6. Swirl in the peanut (or canola) oil to coat.
7. When the first puff of smoke rises, add the shrimp and cook, stirring constantly, for about 2 minutes, or until the shrimp just begin to turn pink.
8. Stir in the veggies (or kimchi), then add the sauce mixture and simmer, stirring constantly, for 1 to 2 minutes, or until the shrimp is just cooked through.
9. Over the noodles, pour the shrimp mixture. Serve with peanuts and scallions on top.
10. Toss everything together at the table before serving.

**Nutritional Information:** (Per Serving)
387 Calories
12 grams of fat
51 grams of carbs
20 grams of protein

**Nutritional Profile:**
Diabetes-appropriate, dairy-free, heart-healthy, healthy pregnancy, high protein, low sodium, low calorie

**Tips:**

Any type of flat wheat noodle can be used for this recipe for the most authentic taste and texture. Seek out a Chinese brand of noodles from an Asian market or a supermarket with a large selection of ingredients used in Chinese cooking.

Dark soy sauce (sometimes called black soy sauce) is thicker than regular soy sauce and has a touch of sweetness. Look for it in Asian markets, or make a substitute by combining a bit of regular soy sauce with a tiny bit of molasses.

Look for Chinese sesame paste similar to tahini with a more prominent roasted sesame flavor in Asian markets. Go for sustainably raised shrimp. Look for shrimp that has received certification from an independent organization, such as the Marine Stewardship Council.

If you can't find certified shrimp, choose wild-caught shrimp from North America; it's more likely to be sustainably caught.

## No. 29: Chipotle Chicken Quinoa Burrito Bowl

This wonderfully flavorful burrito bowl features grilled chicken coated in a spicy chipotle glaze. Loading it with vegetables and using quinoa instead of rice adds nutrition for a much healthier dinner.

**Cook Time:** 30 Minutes

**Overall Time:** 30 Minutes

**Portions:** 4 People

**Produced:** 4 Burrito bowls

**Ingredients:**

- 1 tablespoon chipotle peppers in adobo sauce, finely chopped
- 1 tablespoon olive oil (extra virgin)
- 1/2 teaspoon garlic powder
- 1/2 teaspoon cumin powder
- 1 chicken breast, boneless and skinless
- 1/4 teaspoon salt

- 2 cups quinoa, cooked
- 2 cups romaine lettuce, shredded
- 1 cup rinsed canned pinto beans
- 1/4 cup prepared pico de gallo or other salsa 1 ripe avocado, diced
- 1/4 cup shredded Monterey Jack or Cheddar cheese
- Serving slices of lime

**Directions:**

1. Preheat the grill or broiler to medium-high.
2. In a small bowl, combine the chipotles, oil, garlic powder, and cumin.
3. If broiling, oil the grill rack (see guidelines below) or a rimmed baking sheet. Season the chicken with salt and pepper.
4. Grill the chicken for 5 minutes or broil it for 9 minutes on a baking sheet lined with parchment paper.
5. Continue cooking until an instant-read thermometer inserted in the thickest section registers 165 degrees Fahrenheit, 3 to 5 minutes longer on the grill or 9 minutes more under the broiler.
6. Place on a clean cutting board. Cut into small pieces.
7. 1/2 cup quinoa, 1/2 cup chicken, 1/2 cup lettuce, 1/4 cup beans, 1/4 avocado, 1 tablespoon pico de gallo (or other salsa), and 1 tablespoon cheese go into each burrito bowl.
8. Serve with a wedge of lime.

**Nutritional Information:** (Per Serving)
452 Calories
19 grams of fat
36 grams of carbs
36 grams of protein

**Nutritional Profile:**
Diabetes-appropriate, gluten-free, egg-free, healthy aging, healthy immunity, heart-healthy, high blood pressure, high fiber, high protein, low added

sugars, low sodium, low calorie, nut-free, and soy-free

**Tips:**

To oil a barbecue rack, oil a folded paper towel and rub it over the rack using tongs. Cooking spray should not be used on a hot grill.

**No. 30: Paprika Baked Pork Tenderloin with Potatoes and Broccoli**

You would never believe that this elegant meal comes together on just one baking sheet. While the pork rests, whip together an easy red pepper sauce to complete this truly impressive and healthy dinner. The sauce would also be delicious with chicken. I am willing to bet this easy sheet pan dinner recipe will go into heavy rotation on your kitchen playlist.

**Preparation Time:** 25 Minutes

**Additional Time:** 20 Minutes

**Overall Time:** 45 Minutes

**Portions:** 4 People

**Produced:** 4 Servings

**Ingredients:**

- 3/4 pound Yukon Gold potatoes, cleaned and diced into 1-inch pieces
- 1 medium red onion, peeled and chopped into 1-inch pieces
- 2 tbsp olive oil, divided; 3/4 tsp salt, divided
- 4 cups of broccoli florets (about 1 pound)
- 2 peeled garlic cloves
- 1-1/2 tsp. smoked paprika

- 1/2 tsp. freshly ground pepper, divided
- 2 tsp. Dijon mustard
- 1 pound of trimmed pork tenderloin
- 2 jars (6 oz.) of roasted red bell peppers
- 2 tbsp. low-fat sour cream or plain low-fat Greek yogurt
- 1 tsp. of lemon juice

## Directions:

1. Preheat the oven to 425°F and place a big, rimmed baking sheet in it.
2. In a medium mixing bowl, combine potatoes, onion, 1 tablespoon oil, and 1/4 teaspoon salt; toss to coat.
3. Spray the pan with cooking spray after it has been removed from the oven.
4. Roast for 15 minutes after spreading the potato mixture on the pan.
5. Meanwhile, stir broccoli with 2 teaspoons of olive oil and 1/4 teaspoon salt in a larger mixing bowl.
6. Place the garlic on a small piece of aluminum foil. Fold into a tiny package and drizzle with the remaining 1 teaspoon of oil.
7. In a small bowl, combine paprika, 1/4 teaspoon ground pepper, and the remaining 1/4 teaspoon salt.
8. Cover the pork with mustard. Coat the chicken with the paprika mixture.
9. Take the pan out of the oven.
10. Move the potatoes and onions to one side and set them aside.
11. Place the pork alongside the potatoes, then the broccoli on the opposite side of the pan.
12. Place the garlic packet wherever there is room.
13. Roast for 25 minutes, or until an instant-read thermometer inserted into the thickest part of the pork registers 145 degrees Fahrenheit.
14. Allow the pork to rest while you prepare the sauce.
15. Unwrap the garlic carefully and place it in a tiny food processor or blender.

16. Combine the roasted red peppers, sour cream (or yogurt), lemon juice, and the remaining 1/4 teaspoon ground pepper in a mixing bowl.
17. Blend until smooth.
18. Make 12 slices of pork.
19. Pork, potatoes, and broccoli should be divided among four plates.
20. Drizzle with the red pepper sauce.

**Nutritional Information:** (Per Serving)
323 Calories
10 grams of fat
29 grams of carbs
30 grams of protein

**Nutritional Profile:**
Diabetes-appropriate, gluten-free, egg-free, healthy immunity, healthy aging, high protein, low calorie, nut-free, and soy-free

**In Summary**

This is far from a comprehensive list of type 2 diabetes dinner recipes. I've experimented with these recipes many times over the years, mixing and matching, and I encourage you to do the same. Make these supper recipes to fit your specific needs.

In addition, I recommend that you use these dinner recipes to plan your meals with the planners that I have included. Enjoy!

# 9

# Dessert Recipes

C an a type 2 diabetic eat sugary foods? We should look into this further and see whether we can consume desserts. If you have type 2 diabetes, eating sweet pastries might trigger a significant jump in your blood glucose levels.

Is this to say that enjoying a sweet treat is completely forbidden? Fortunately, that is not the case. Because the presence of sugar in desserts does not imply that a diabetic should avoid them entirely,

In any event, no food is completely out of reach; to keep glucose levels low, it is critical to limit eating delicacies that include primarily refined carbs and sugar, for example, snack cakes, candies, or treats.

To combat this, we should consume sweets rich in fiber, protein, and healthy fats, which will aid in slowing our glucose reaction. If your sweets lack those components, there are still ways to incorporate them into a nice feast or snack.

Everything relies on having the appropriate balance of nutrients to keep your glucose levels stable. Most of us recognize that most goodies are manufactured with a lot more sugar, and since controlling glucose levels is critical for someone with diabetes, it appears that these types of sweet food sources would be a huge mix-up for a diabetic to consume.

Diabetes is a very common condition among Americans; more than 37 million people have diabetes, and that number is growing, and one out of every three Americans has prediabetes, according to the Communities for Infectious Prevention and Control.

With so many people striving to figure out how to effectively manage their glucose levels for greater well-being, it's vital to figure out how to eat to keep those spikes low while still engaging in a tasty pleasure.

So, how does a diabetic enjoy the desert without fear of elevated glucose levels? Matching a high-sugar dessert with a protein or fiber item can help reduce sugar retention in the circulatory system and prevent glucose spikes.

This is because protein and fiber take substantially longer to digest than simple carbs like table sugar or high fructose corn syrup. For example, if you're having a treat, you might want to pair it with a small handful of nuts or a fiber-rich natural product.

That being said, the healthiest types of treats for diabetics to eat are those that now combine these components and are typically lower in sugar, such as natural products with cream, yogurt-based desserts, and pastries with nuts or nut margarine.

I've included some of my favorite treat recipes that are simple to create, healthy, and, when done correctly, will satisfy our collective sugar cravings. As a side note, these dessert recipes should be consumed in moderation.

**No. 1: Blueberry Lemon Energy Balls**

Blueberries are my all-time favorite berries, and when I need a late-morning pick-me-up, these overwhelming blueberry lemon balls come together in minutes and are the ultimate on-the-go snack. Pecans boost plant-based protein and will help you stay empowered, while maple syrup adds a nice touch.

**Cook Time:** 10 Minutes

**Overall Time:** 10 Minutes

**Portions:** 6

**Produced:** 6 Servings

**Ingredients:**

- Walnuts, 3/4 cup
- 1/2 cup of pitted dates
- 1/4 cup of dried blueberries
- Old-fashioned rolled oats, 3/4 cup
- 2 tablespoons of undiluted maple syrup
- 1 tablespoon of lemon juice and 1 teaspoon of grated lemon zest

**Directions:**

1. In a food processor, blend the blueberries, dates, and walnuts after adding them. Process for 7 to 10 seconds.
2. Add the lemon juice, maple syrup, and oats. Continue processing for another 20 to 30 seconds or until a thick, smooth paste forms.
3. Transfer the paste to a small bowl, then stir in the lemon zest.
4. Form and roll the mixture into 18 little balls with the palms of your hands.

**Nutritional Information** (per serving)

190 Calories

9 grams of fat

27 grams of carbs

4 grams of protein

**Nutritional Profile:**

Diabetes-appropriate, dairy-free, egg-free, gluten-free, soy-free, heart-healthy, vegan, vegetarian

**Tips:**

To save for later: Refrigerate in an airtight container for up to 2 weeks.

**No. 2: Strawberry Chocolate Greek Yogurt Bark**

This gently upgraded Greek yogurt is studded with young strawberries and chocolate chips before being frozen into lumps that resemble chocolate bark but are far superior. This gorgeous bite, or sound pastry, is great for both children and adults. To ensure the creamiest bark possible, use full-fat yogurt.

**Preparation Time:** 10 Minutes

**Extra Time:** 3 Hours

**Overall Time:** 3 Hours, 10 Minutes

**Portions:** 32

**Produced:** 32 Pieces

**Ingredients:**

- Greek yogurt is made with three cups of full milk.
- 1/4 cup of pure honey or maple syrup
- Vanilla extract, 1 teaspoon
- Sliced strawberries in 1-1/2 cups
- Mini chocolate chips, 1/4 cup

## Directions:

1. Use parchment paper to line a baking sheet with a rim.
2. In a medium bowl, combine yogurt, maple syrup (or honey), and vanilla.
3. Spread into a 10-by-15-inch rectangle on the baking sheet that has been prepared.
4. Add the strawberries and chocolate chips to the surface.
5. Freeze for at least 3 hours, or until very stiff.
6. Cut or split into 32 pieces to serve.

**Equipment:** Parchment paper

## Nutritional Information (per serving)
34 Calories
1 gram of fat
4 grams of carbs
2 grams of protein

## Nutritional Profile:
Diabetes-appropriate, gluten-free, egg-free, nut-free, heart-healthy, low-calorie, low-carbohydrate, low-fat, low-sodium, vegetarian

## Tips:

To save for later: Freeze airtight between sheets of parchment for up to 1 month; let stand at room temperature for 15 minutes before serving.

## No. 3: Cranberry Almond Granola Bars

There are so many granola bar choices at your nearby supermarket, but at the same time, they're really simple and a lot better to make at home. On the other hand, you can add any blend of little (or slashed) dried natural products, nuts, seeds, and chocolate chips for the dried cranberries and nuts in this adaptation; the decision is yours.

**Preparation Time:** 20 Minutes

**Extra Time:** 1 Hour, 10 Minutes

**Overall Time:** 1 Hour, 30 Minutes

**Portions**

**Produced:** 24 Bars

**Ingredients:**

- Three cups of traditional rolled oats
- A single cup of crispy brown rice cereal
- 1 cup of cranberries, dried
- 1/2 cup chopped, roasted almonds
- 1/2 cup chopped, toasted pecans
- 1/4 teaspoon of salt
- 2/3 cup light corn syrup or brown rice syrup
- 1/2 cup of smooth almond butter
- Vanilla extract, 1 teaspoon

**Directions:**

1. Set the oven's temperature to 325 F.

2. Using parchment paper, line a 9 by 13-inch baking sheet, with excess parchment hanging over both edges.
3. Spray some cooking spray on the parchment paper lightly.
4. In a large bowl, mix the oats, rice cereal, cranberries, almonds, pecans, and salt.
5. Mix the rice syrup (or corn syrup), almond butter, and vanilla in a bowl that can go in the microwave.
6. 30 seconds in the microwave (or 1 minute in a saucepan over medium heat).
7. Add the dry ingredients and blend thoroughly by stirring.
8. Use the back of a spatula to transfer to the prepared pan and press firmly into the pan.
9. For chewier bars, bake for 20 to 25 minutes, or until the edges are just beginning to color but the center is still soft.
10. Bake for 30 to 35 minutes until the edges are golden brown and the centers are still somewhat gooey for crunchier bars. (Both remain soft when warm and become firmer as they cool.)
11. Allow it to cool in the pan for ten minutes, then—while it's still soft—lift it out of the pan and onto a cutting board with the aid of the parchment.
12. Cut into 24 bars, then allow them to chill for a further 30 minutes without separating the bars.
13. After cooling, cut into bars.

**Equipment:** Parchment paper

**Nutritional Information** (per serving)
161 Calories
7 grams of fat
23 grams of carbs
3 grams of protein

**Nutritional Profile:**
Diabetes-appropriate, dairy-free, egg-free, gluten-free, soy-free, heart-

healthy, healthy pregnancy, high fiber, low sodium, low calorie, vegan, vegetarian

**Tips:**

To keep for later: Wrap individually in plastic wrap and store at room temperature for up to a week.

### No. 4: Air Fryer Crispy Chickpeas

In the summer of 2021, I purchased an air fryer, and I love it. These air-seared chickpea snacks are strongly seasoned and inconceivably crunchy. Drying the chickpeas is expected to give them a great crunch, so kindly don't skirt this step. If you have time, leave them on the counter to dry for a little while before broiling.

**Preparation Time:** 20 Minutes

**Overall Time:** 20 Minutes

**Portions:** 4

**Produced:** 1 cup

**Ingredients:**

- 1 (15-ounce) can of rinsed and drained unsalted chickpeas
- toasted sesame oil, 1-1/2 tablespoons
- smoked paprika, 1/4 teaspoon
- 1/4 teaspoon of red pepper flakes
- 1/8 teaspoon of salt
- Nonstick cooking Spray
- 2 lime wedges

## Directions:

1. On multiple layers of paper towels, spread the chickpeas.
2. Roll the chickpeas beneath the paper towels to dry them on all sides, then add additional paper towels on top and pat them until extremely dry.
3. In a medium bowl, mix the oil and chickpeas.
4. Salt, crushed red pepper, and paprika should be added.
5. Pour into a cooking spray-coated air fryer basket.
6. Cook for 12 to 14 minutes at 400 degrees Fahrenheit, shaking the basket occasionally, until very nicely browned.
7. Serve the chickpeas with lime wedges on top.

## Nutritional Information (per serving)

132 Calories

6 grams of fat

14 grams of carbs

5 grams of protein

## Nutritional Profile:

Diabetes-appropriate, dairy-free, egg-free, gluten-free, nut-free, soy-free, heart-healthy, high fiber, low carbohydrate, low sodium, low calorie, vegan, vegetarian

## No. 5: Air Fryer Sweet Potato Chips

These potato chips are delicious when done correctly. This meal is really simple to prepare and nutritionally healthy. In the air fryer, the meagerly chopped yams cook to a hard mash. These locally produced chips also use significantly less oil, which eliminates calories and fat, making them excellent for diabetics. They are typically a sweet side for sandwiches, burgers, and wraps, but the possibilities are endless.

**Preparation Time:** 5 Minutes

**Extra Time:** 55 Minutes

**Overall Time:** 1 Hour

**Portions:** 8

**Produced:** 8 Servings

**Ingredients:**

- 8 ounces of one medium sweet potato, cut into rounds that are 1/8 inch thick.
- Canola oil, 1 tablespoon
- 1/4 teaspoon ground pepper, 1/4 teaspoon sea salt

**Directions:**

1. Slices of sweet potato should soak for 20 minutes in a big bowl of cold water.
2. Using paper towels, wipe the drain and dry it.
3. Sweet potatoes should be put back in the dry bowl.
4. Salt, pepper, and oil to taste; gently toss to coat.
5. Spray some cooking spray on the air fryer basket lightly.
6. Just enough sweet potatoes should be arranged in the basket to create one layer.
7. Cook for 15 minutes at 350 degrees Fahrenheit, rotating and rearranging into a single layer every 5 minutes, until well cooked and crispy.
8. Carefully transfer the chips from the air fryer to a platter using tongs.
9. The remaining sweet potatoes should be repeated.
10. Give the chips five minutes to cool.
11. Serve right away, or let it cool fully and keep for up to three days in an

airtight plastic jar.

**Nutritional Information** (per serving)

31 Calories

2 grams of fat

4 grams of carbs

0 grams of protein

**Nutritional Profile:**

Diabetes-appropriate, dairy-free, egg-free, gluten-free, nut-free, soy-free, heart-healthy, low carbohydrate, low fat, low sodium, low calorie, vegan, vegetarian

**Tips:**

To keep for later: Store in an airtight plastic container for up to 3 days.

**No. 6: Crispy Peanut Butter Balls**

Can you believe that these firm peanut butter balls that both kids and adults will adore require only four basic ingredients? Make this easy recipe for a small treat, a quick snack, or a small custom-made gift. Swap the peanut butter for almond margarine or sunflower seed spread for a nut-free snack.

**Preparation Time:** 15 Minutes

**Extra Time:** 30 Minutes

**Overall Time:** 45 Minutes

**Portions:** 12

**Produced:** 12 Servings

**Ingredients:**

- 1/2 cup natural almond, peanut, or sunflower seed butter
- 3/4 cup of crispy rice cereal
- Pure maple syrup, 1 teaspoon
- 1/2 cup melted dark chocolate chips (see tips below.)

**Directions:**

1. Use wax paper or parchment to line a baking pan.
2. In a medium bowl, mix the cereal, peanut butter, and maple syrup.
3. Make 12 balls out of the mixture, using about 2 tablespoons per ball.
4. Place them on the prepared baking sheet.
5. The balls should be frozen for around 15 minutes, or until hard.
6. In melted chocolate, roll the balls.
7. Once the chocolate has set (around 15 minutes), return it to the freezer.

**Nutritional Information** (per serving)
112 Calories
8 grams of fat
8 grams of carbs
3 grams of protein

**Nutritional Profile:**
Diabetes-appropriate, dairy-free, egg-free, gluten-free, soy-free, heart-healthy, low-calorie, low-carbohydrate, low-sodium, vegan

**Tips:**

To keep for later: Refrigerate in an airtight container for up to 3 weeks.

To serve: Melt chocolate in the microwave on medium for 1 minute. Stir, then continue microwaving on medium, stirring every 20 seconds, until melted.

Or place chocolate in the top of a double boiler over hot, but not boiling, water. Stir until melted. Enjoy!

## No. 6: Lemon Parm Popcorn

Bring your popcorn back to life with a bit of lemon pepper and Parmesan cheese.

**Cook Time:** 5 Minutes

**Overall Time:** 5 Minutes

**Portions:** 2

**Produced:** 2 servings

**Ingredients:**

- Extra virgin olive oil, 2 teaspoons
- 1/2 teaspoon of lemon pepper
- A dash of salt
- Air-popped popcorn in three cups
- Freshly grated Parmesan cheese, 1 tablespoon

**Directions:**

1. In a small bowl, combine the oil, salt, and lemon pepper.
2. The popcorn should be drizzled over and then coated.
3. Serve right away after adding Parmesan.

**Nutritional Information** (per serving)
99 Calories
6 grams of fat

10 grams of carbs

2 grams of protein

**Nutritional Profile:**

Diabetes-appropriate, dairy-free, gluten-free, heart-healthy, low in added sugars, low in carbohydrates, low in sodium, low in calories, vegetarian

**No. 7: Avocado and Salsa Cracker**

For a fiery Southwest-inspired garnish on whole grain crispbread, try this avocado and salsa snack, which is full of fiber, veggies, and healthy fats and takes only minutes to make.

**Preparation Time:** 10 Minutes

**Overall Time:** 10 Minutes

**Portions:** 1

**Produced:** 1 Crispbread with topping

**Ingredients:**

- 1/8 avocado
- 1 large crispbread, preferably Wasa® Sourdough Whole Grain Crispbread.
- 1 tablespoon of low-sodium salsa
- 1 tablespoon of cilantro for garnish

**Directions:**

1. Spread the mashed avocado on the crispbread after mashing the avocado in a small bowl.

2. Add salsa on top.
3. If desired, add cilantro as a garnish.

**Nutritional Information** (per serving)
76 Calories
4 grams of fat
10 grams of carbs
1 gram of protein

**Nutritional Profile:**
Diabetes-appropriate, egg-free, nut-free, soy-free, high fiber, low calorie, low carbohydrate, low sodium, vegan, vegetarian

**Tips:**

Look for crackers with 100 to 140 calories per serving, less than 20 grams of carbohydrates, at least 3 grams of fiber, 2 grams of saturated fat or less, and less than 200 mg of salt.

**No. 8: Chile-Lime Peanuts**

Roused and sold by roadside vendors across Mexico. These peanuts are spicy, but if you can find salted peanuts, skip the salt. If you need more flavor, use the most extreme amount of cayenne pepper.

**Cook Time:** 5 Minutes

**Extra Time:** 45 Minutes

**Overall Time:** 50 Minutes

**Portions:** 48

**Produced:** 6 Cups

**Ingredients:**

- Juice from 6 tablespoons of limes
- Chili powder, 6 tablespoons
- Kosher salt, 4 teaspoons
- Cayenne pepper, 1/2 to 1 teaspoon
- 6 cups of cocktail peanuts, unsalted

**Directions:**

1. The oven should be preheated to 250 degrees Fahrenheit. Place racks in the upper and lower thirds of the oven.
2. In a large bowl, combine lime juice, cayenne, salt, and chili powder.
3. Add the peanuts and coat well.
4. Spread evenly on two large-rimmed baking pans. Divide.
5. Bake for about 45 minutes, stirring every 15 minutes, until dry.
6. Allow it to be cool.
7. Use an airtight container for storage.

**Nutritional Information** (per serving)
111 Calories
9 grams of fat
5 grams of carbs
5 grams of protein

**Nutritional Profile:**
Diabetes-appropriate, dairy-free, gluten-free, heart-healthy, low in added sugars, low in sodium, low in calories, low in carbohydrates, vegan, vegetarian

**Tips:**

To keep for later: Store in an airtight container for up to 3 weeks.

No more washing dishes: A rimmed baking sheet is great for everything from roasting to catching accidental drips and spills. For effortless cleanup and to keep your baking sheets in tip-top shape, line them with a layer of foil before each use.

**No. 9: Cinnamon Popcorn**

This super simple spiced popcorn snack will satisfy your sugar cravings and provide a healthy dose of whole grains, fiber, and antioxidants.

**Preparation Time:** 10 Minutes

**Extra Time:** 5 Minutes

**Overall Time:** 15 Minutes

**Portions:** 4

**Produced:** 4 Servings

**Ingredients:**

- Popped popcorn in 8 cups
- Sugar, 2 teaspoons (see tips below)
- 1/2 teaspoon of cinnamon powder
- Nonstick cooking spray, butter-flavored

**Directions:**

1. Set the oven to 350 degrees Fahrenheit.
2. If desired, line a shallow roasting pan with foil.

3. In the shallow roasting pan, spread the popcorn.
4. Cinnamon and sugar should be combined in a small bowl.
5. Cooking spray should be used sparingly, and popcorn should be evenly coated.
6. Add the cinnamon mixture and toss once more to properly distribute.
7. About 5 minutes, or just until crisp, should be baked.

**Nutritional Information** (per serving)
71 Calories
1 gram of fat
15 grams of carbs
2 grams of protein

**Nutritional Profile:**
Diabetes-appropriate, dairy-free,egg-free, gluten-free, nut-free, soy-free, heart-healthy, low-calorie, low-carbohydrate, low-fat, low-sodium, vegan, vegetarian

**Tips:**

If using a sugar substitute, choose Splenda (R) Granular, Equal (R) Spoonfuls or packets, or Sweet 'N Low (R) packets or bulk in place of granulated sugar. Be sure to follow package directions to use a product amount that's equivalent to 2 teaspoons of granulated sugar. Nutrition Facts Per Serving: same as above except for 63 calories and 13 grams of carbohydrates.

**No. 10: Cherry, Cocoa, and Pistachio Energy Balls**

The blend of minced dried cherries and pistachios makes these energy balls a pungent, sweet nibble to fulfill every one of your desires. Almond spread and cocoa add substance and chocolaty allure. Serve any season of the day as a bite or sweet.

**Preparation Time:** 25 Minutes

**Overall Time:** 25 Minutes

**Portions:** 32

**Produced:** 32 Balls

**Ingredients:**

- Dried cherries, 1-1/2 cups
- 3/4 cup salted and shelled pistachios
- 1/2 cup of almond butter
- Cocoa powder, 3 tablespoons
- Maple syrup only, 4 tablespoons
- 1/2 teaspoon of cinnamon powder

**Directions:**

1. In a food processor, mash cherries, pistachios, almond butter, cocoa powder, maple syrup, and cinnamon.
2. When the mixture is crumbly but can be squeezed into a cohesive ball, process for 10 to 20 pulses to finely chop the ingredients. After that, process for about a minute, scraping down the sides as needed.
3. About 1 tablespoon of the mixture should be squeezed tightly between your palms before being rolled into a ball with damp hands (to prevent the mixture from sticking to them).
4. Put it in a plastic container for storage.
5. The remaining mixture could be used again.

**Nutritional Information** (per serving)
72 Calories
4 grams of fat

9 grams of carbs

2 grams of protein

**Nutritional Profile:**

Diabetes-appropriate, dairy-free, egg-free, gluten-free, soy-free, heart-healthy, low-calorie, low sodium, low carbohydrate, low added sugars, vegan, vegetarian

**Tips:**

To keep for later: Refrigerate for up to 1 week or freeze for up to 3 months.

### No. 11: Blueberry Cashew Granola Bars

Coconut extract imparts a tropical flavor to these custom-made granola bars. Change out the blueberries, cashews, and flaxseeds for any combination of your favorite dried natural goods, nuts, or seeds. I experimented with several sugars, including maple syrup and honey, but found that earthy-colored rice syrup held the bars together the best.

**Preparation Time:** 20 Minutes

**Extra Time:** 1 Hour, 10 Minutes

**Overall Time:** 1 Hour, 30 Minutes

**Portions:** 1

**Produced:** 24 Bars

**Ingredients:**

- Traditional rolled oats in three cups

- 1 cup of crispy brown rice cereal
- 1 cup of dried blueberries
- 1/2 cup chopped, roasted cashews, unsalted
- 1/2 cup of toasted flaxseed and 1/4 teaspoon of salt
- 2/3 cup brown rice syrup or light corn syrup
- 1/2 cup of cashew butter
- 1 teaspoon of coconut extract

## Directions:

1. Set the oven's temperature to 325 F.
2. Using parchment paper, line a 9 by 13-inch baking sheet with excess parchment hanging over both edges.
3. Spray some cooking spray on the parchment paper lightly.
4. In a sizable mixing bowl, combine the oats, rice cereal, blueberries, cashews, flaxseed, and salt.
5. Mix the rice syrup (or corn syrup), cashew butter, and coconut extract in a bowl that can go in the microwave.
6. 30 seconds in the microwave (or 1 minute in a saucepan over medium heat).
7. Add the dry ingredients and blend thoroughly by stirring.
8. Use the back of a spatula to transfer to the prepared pan and press firmly into the pan.
9. For chewier bars, bake for 20 to 25 minutes, or until the edges are just beginning to color but the center is still soft.
10. Bake for 30 to 35 minutes, until the edges are golden brown and the centers are still somewhat gooey for crunchier bars. (Both remain soft when warm and become firmer as they cool.)
11. Allow it to cool in the pan for ten minutes, then—while it's still soft—lift it out of the pan and onto a cutting board with the aid of the parchment.
12. Cut into 24 bars, then allow them to chill for a further 30 minutes without separating the bars.
13. After cooling, cut into bars.

**Nutritional Information** (per serving)

165 Calories

7 grams of fat

25 grams of carbs

3 grams of protein

**Nutritional Profile:**

Diabetes-appropriate, dairy-free, egg-free, soy-free, gluten-free, heart-healthy, healthy pregnancy, high fiber, low calorie, low sodium, vegan, vegetarian

**Tips:**

To save for later, individually wrap in airtight plastic wrap and store at room temperature for up to a week.

**No. 12: Cream Cheese Dip and Crackers**

Slipping green peppers into this speedy, fresh dip supplies added vitamin C.

**Preparation Time:** 5 Minutes

**Overall Time:** 5 Minutes

**Portions:** 4

**Produced:** 4 Servings

**Ingredients:**

- A half-cup of low-fat cream cheese
- Green bell pepper, minced, 1/4 cup
- 2 tablespoons of pecans, chopped

- 1/4 cup of crushed, drained pineapple
- 40 Mini Triscuit Crackers

**Directions:**

1. Cream cheese, pepper, pecans, and pineapple are all combined.
2. Served with crackers.

**Nutritional Information** (per serving)
162 Calories
9 grams of fat
16 grams of carbs
4 grams of protein

**Nutritional Profile:**
Diabetes-appropriate, soy-free, egg-free, low-calorie, low-sodium, vegetarian

**No. 13: Yogurt with Blueberries**

Blueberries add all the pleasantness you want to a protein-rich Greek yogurt in this delightful tidbit.

**Preparation Time:** 5 Minutes

**Overall Time:** 5 Minutes

**Portions:** 1

**Produced:** 1 Serving

**Ingredients:**

- 1 cup plain, nonfat Greek yogurt
- Blueberries, 1/4 cup

**Directions:**

Blueberries should be added on top of the yogurt in a bowl. Nothing to it, enjoy!

**Nutritional Information** (per serving)

154 Calories

1 gram of fat

14 grams of carbs

23 grams of protein

**Nutritional Profile:**

Diabetes-appropriate, egg-free, nut-free, soy-free, gluten-free, heart-healthy, healthy aging, bone health, high calcium, low calorie, low carbohydrate, low fat, low sodium, vegetarian

**No. 14: Roasted Buffalo Chickpeas**

Before cooking, soak the chickpeas in vinegary hot sauce to give them a wonderful tang. What was the result? A deliciously crispy nibble that is also good for you.

**Preparation Time:** 5 Minutes

**Extra Time:** 30 Minutes

**Overall Time:** 35 Minutes

**Portions:** 4

**Produced:** 4 Servings

**Ingredients:**

- White vinegar, 1 tbsp
- Cayenne pepper, to taste, 1/2 teaspoon
- 1/4 teaspoon of salt
- 1 (15-ounce) can of washed chickpeas, no salt added

**Directions:**

1. The oven rack should be in the upper third; heat to 400 degrees Fahrenheit.
2. Salt, cayenne, and vinegar are combined in a large bowl.
3. The chickpeas should be completely dried before being mixed with the vinegar mixture.
4. Spread on a baking sheet with a rim.
5. For 30 to 35 minutes, roast the chickpeas, tossing twice, until they are crisp and golden.
6. The chickpeas will get crisp as they cool if you let them cool for 30 minutes on the pan.

**Nutritional Information** (per serving)
109 Calories
1 gram of fat
18 grams of carbs
6 grams of protein

**Nutritional Profile:**
Diabetes-appropriate, dairy-free, egg-free, gluten-free, soy-free, nut-free, heart-healthy, high fiber, low fat, low sodium, low calorie, vegan, vegetarian

**Tips:**

Make ahead of time: Chickpeas keep crisp at room temperature for 2 to 4 hours; if stored longer, re-crisp at 400 degrees Fahrenheit for 5 to 10 minutes.

**No. 15: Seneca White Corn No-Bake Energy Balls**

These no-bake energy balls get loads of resilience from a blend of oats and corn flour, peanut butter, coconut, and dried leafy foods and nuts. They're effectively adaptable by switching around the dried leafy foods.

**Cook Time:** 15 Minutes

**Overall Time:** 15 Minutes

**Portions:** 36

**Produced:** 36 Servings

**Ingredients:**

- 1-1/2 cups of quick oats
- 1 cup of roasted white corn flour (see tips below)
- 1 teaspoon of cinnamon powder
- 1 teaspoon of salt
- Natural peanut butter, half a cup
- 1/4 cup unsweetened applesauce
- 2 tablespoons of pure maple syrup
- Water, 2 tablespoons
- Honey, 2 tablespoons
- Vanilla extract, 1 teaspoon
- 1/2 cup of unsweetened coconut flakes plus some more for rolling
- 1/2 cup dried fruit, such as currants or raisins
- 1/2 cup chopped unsalted, roasted, mixed nuts, such as pecans, almonds, walnuts, and/or hazelnuts

## Directions:

1. Use parchment paper to cover a baking sheet.
2. In a medium bowl, mix the oats, corn flour, cinnamon, and salt.
3. Add the peanut butter, applesauce, maple syrup, honey, vanilla, and 2 tablespoons of water.
4. Add the nuts, dried fruit, and coconut flakes slowly and gently.
5. Roll the mixture into 1-inch balls with clean hands, using about 1 heaping tablespoon for each. Stir in 1 tablespoon of water if the mixture is too dry to roll.
6. If preferred, roll in extra coconut.

## Nutritional Information (per serving)

77 Calories

4 grams of fat

9 grams of carbs

2 grams of protein

## Nutritional Profile:

Diabetes-appropriate, dairy-free, egg-free, soy-free, gluten-free, heart-healthy, low-sodium, vegan, vegetarian

## Tips:

You can buy roasted white corn flour from Gakwi:yo:h Farms online at shop.senecamuseum.org.

## No. 16: Baked Broccoli Cheddar Quinoa Bites

These delectable muffin-like quinoa pieces are low in carbs and high in protein; as an additional bonus, you'll enjoy their cheesy flavor.

**Preparation Time:** 20 Minutes

**Extra Time:** 45 Minutes

**Overall Time:** 1 Hour, 5 Minutes

**Portions:** 8

**Produced:** 16 Bites

**Ingredients:**

- 1/2 cup of quinoa
- 1/4 teaspoon divided and 1/8 teaspoon of salt
- 3/4 cup broccoli, chopped finely
- 3/4 cup of cheddar cheese, shredded
- 1/2 teaspoon of baking powder
- 1/2 teaspoon of garlic powder
- 1/4 cup onion powder
- 1/4 teaspoon of pepper, ground
- Lightly beaten, one large egg
- Nonstick cooking Spray

**Directions:**

1. Set the oven to 350 degrees Fahrenheit.
2. A 24-cup mini muffin pan can have 16 cups lined with paper liners (see suggestions below) or sprayed with cooking spray.
3. As directed on the packaging, prepare the quinoa with 1/8 teaspoon of salt.
4. Remove from heat and allow it to stand for five minutes, covered.
5. Let cool for at least 10 minutes before transferring to a large bowl.
6. The remaining 1/4 teaspoon of salt, pepper, baking soda, garlic powder, onion powder, broccoli, and cheddar are all added to the quinoa. Add the egg and stir.

7. To distribute the quinoa mixture among the prepared muffin cups, briefly moisten your fingers and press down firmly.
8. Spray some cooking spray on the tops.
9. Bake for 22 to 25 minutes, or until brown.
10. Allow to cool for 20 minutes in the pan on a wire rack, then transfer to the rack to finish cooling.
11. Quinoa with 1/4 teaspoon of salt, add the egg and stir.
12. To distribute the quinoa mixture among the prepared muffin cups, briefly moisten your fingers and press down firmly.
13. Spray some cooking spray on the tops.
14. Bake for 22 to 25 minutes, or until brown.
15. Allow to cool for 20 minutes in the pan on a wire rack, then transfer to the rack to finish cooling.

**Equipment:** mini muffin pan (24-cup)

**Nutritional Information** (per serving)
   87 Calories
   4 grams of fat
   8 grams of carbs
   5 grams of protein

**Nutritional Profile:**
   Diabetes-appropriate, gluten-free, nut-free, soy-free, heart-healthy, low in added sugars, low in carbohydrates, low in sodium, low in calories, vegetarian

**Tips:**

To prevent sticking, refrigerate the cooked bits for at least 2 hours before removing them from the liners if using paper liners.

To save for later: Refrigerate for up to 3 days.

## No. 17: Savory Date and Pistachio Bites

A hint of sweetness from the dates and raisins, along with crunch and nuttiness from the pistachios, make these nibbles great for a quick snack or as an addition to a cheese board.

**Preparation Time:** 10 Minutes

**Overall Time:** 10 Minutes

**Portions:** 32

**Produced:** 32 Servings

**Ingredients:**

- 2 cups of whole, pitted dates
- 1 cup shelled, raw, and unsalted pistachios
- Golden raisins, 1 cup
- 1 teaspoon of fennel seeds, ground
- 1/4 teaspoon of ground pepper

**Directions:**

1. In a food processor, combine dates, pistachios, raisins, fennel, and pepper.
2. Process until very finely chopped.
3. Make approximately 32 balls using about one tablespoon each.

**Nutritional Information** (per serving)
68 Calories
2 grams of fat
13 grams of carbs

1 gram of protein

**Nutritional Profile:**

Diabetes-appropriate, dairy-free, egg-free, gluten-free, soy-free, heart-healthy, low in added sugars, low in carbohydrate, low in fat, low in sodium, low in calories, vegan, vegetarian

**Tips:**

To prepare ahead of time: Store it airtight at room temperature for up to 3 hours.

**No. 18: Apricot-Ginger Energy Balls**

This simple energy ball utilizes regular fixings to provide you with a light meal of energy when you want it. Dried apricots and honey keep the coconut and oats intact, while ginger and tahini develop sweet flavors. Prepared in only 25 minutes, you can have these as an in-and-out breakfast, evening tidbit, or sweet treat after supper.

**Preparation Time:** 25 Minutes

**Overall Time:** 25 Minutes

**Portions:** 32

**Produced:** 32 Balls

**Ingredients:**

- Apricots, dry, in 1-1/2 cups
- 1/4 cup finely shredded unsweetened coconut 1/4 cup rolled oats
- Tahini, 6 tablespoons

- Honey, 3 tablespoons
- 3/4 teaspoon of ginger powder
- A dash of salt

**Directions:**

1. In a food processor, combine apricots, oats, coconut, tahini, honey, ginger, and salt.
2. When the mixture is crumbly but can be squeezed into a cohesive ball, process for 10 to 20 pulses to finely chop the ingredients. After that, process for about a minute, scraping down the sides as needed.
3. About 1 tablespoon of the mixture should be squeezed tightly between your palms before being rolled into a ball with damp hands (to prevent the mixture from sticking to them).
4. Put it in a plastic container for storage.
5. The remaining mixture can be used again.

**Nutritional Information** (per serving)

57 Calories

3 grams of fat

8 grams of carbs

1 gram of protein

**Nutritional Profile:**

Diabetes-appropriate, dairy-free, egg-free, gluten-free, nut-free, heart-healthy, low in added sugars, low in carbohydrate, low in fat, low in sodium, low in calories, vegetarian

**Tips:**

To save for later: Refrigerate for up to 1 week or freeze for up to 3 months.

**No. 19: Mojito Blueberry and Watermelon Salad**

This joyful and sturdy organic product salad gets a punch from rum, lime, and mint thanks to the excellent mojito mixed drink. The discretionary piment d'Espelette, a sweet, hot ground pepper from the Basque district of France, adds a smidgen of intensity that is a pleasant differentiation to the sweet organic product.

Search for this flavor at specialty stores, all around loaded markets, or on the web. You could likewise trade in chile lime preparation mix (like Tajn) for a comparative unpretentious kick or discard the zest through and through.

Go ahead and avoid the rum on the off chance that you incline toward a liquor-free serving of mixed greens. Regardless of the rum, this salad has a mid-year lawn barbecue on top of it.

**Preparation Time:** 10 Minutes

**Extra Time:** 10 Minutes

**Overall Time:** 20 Minutes

**Portions:** 6

**Produced:** 7 ½ Cups

**Ingredients:**

- 1 tablespoon of rum
- 1 lime's zest
- 1 teaspoon of lime juice
- 1/8 tsp. of salt
- Piment d'espelette, 1/4 teaspoon (optional)
- 6 cups of watermelon cubes
- Blueberries, 1 cup

- 1/4 cup chopped mint
- Lime wedges

**Directions:**

1. In a large bowl, mix the rum with the lime zest, lime juice, salt, and piment d'espelette (if using).
2. Toss in the watermelon, blueberries, and mint before serving.
3. Allow to stand for at least 10 minutes before serving (or cover and chill for up to two hours).
4. Before serving, stir.

**Nutritional Information** (per serving)

68 Calories

0 grams of fat

16 grams of carbs

1 gram of protein

**Nutritional Profile:**

Diabetes-appropriate, dairy-free, egg-free, gluten-free, nut-free, soy-free, heart-healthy, healthy immunity, low fat, low sodium, low calorie, vegan, vegetarian

**Tips:**

To save for later: Refrigerate for up to 2 hours.

**No. 20: Baked Parsnip Chips**

These parsnip chips have just four fixings and couldn't be more straightforward to make. They're best when the parsnips are cut meagerly and equally, so if you have a mandoline, this would be the ideal chance to get them out.

**Preparation Time:** 15 Minutes

**Extra Time:** 1 Hour

**Overall Time:** 1 Hour, 15 Minutes

**Portions:** 12

**Produced:** 4 Cups

**Ingredients:**

- 6 cups of very thinly cut parsnips, 2 pounds
- 1/2 teaspoon of salt and 1/4 cup canola oil
- 1/2 teaspoon of ground pepper

**Directions:**

1. Oven rack placement should be in the middle and lower thirds. The temperature should be 350 degrees Fahrenheit.
2. Parsnips should be mixed with oil, salt, and pepper in a large bowl.
3. Spread into even layers and divide across two baking sheets.
4. About an hour will be needed to bake the parsnips until they are golden brown, stirring them occasionally and flipping the pans from back to front halfway through.

**Equipment:** Mandoline or waffle cutter

**Nutritional Information** (per serving)
90 Calories
5 grams of fat
12 grams of carbs
1 gram of protein

**Nutritional Profile:**

Diabetes-appropriate, egg-free, nut-free, gluten-free, soy-free, heart-healthy, high fiber, low carbohydrate, low calorie, vegan, vegetarian

### No. 21: Homemade Multi-Seed Crackers

Turn extra earthy-colored rice and quinoa from supper or feast preparation into these delicious fresh wafers that are stacked with three great-for-you seeds and make an everything bagel flavor, without the bagel. The entire grains that make up this copycat saltine recipe add loads of fiber for a solid bite that matches impeccably with hummus or cheddar.

**Preparation Time:** 25 Minutes

**Extra Time:** 35 Minutes

**Overall Time:** 1 Hour

**Portions:** 24

**Produced:** 24 Crackers

**Ingredients:**

- 1 cup of warm brown rice that has been cooked
- 1 cup of cooked, at room temperature, quinoa
- 1/4 cup flaxseeds, 1/4 cup sesame seeds
- Sunflower seeds, 1/4 cup
- 2 tablespoons of tamari with a low sodium content
- Water, 2 tablespoons
- 1/4 teaspoon each of salt and ground pepper

**Directions:**

1. In the upper and lower parts of the oven, install oven racks.
2. Heat to 350 degrees Fahrenheit.
3. Sized to fit three big baking sheets, cut three pieces of parchment paper.
4. In a food processor, combine rice, quinoa, sesame seeds, flaxseeds, sunflower seeds, tamari, water, salt, and pepper.
5. Process until the mixture is well-combined and has become finely chopped.
6. It's going to be sticky dough.
7. The dough is divided in half. Between two sheets of the prepared parchment paper, sandwich one piece of dough.
8. Spread as thinly as you can.
9. The dough should be put on a baking sheet after the top parchment sheet has been removed.
10. The remaining dough and prepared parchment should be used again.
11. For 15 minutes, bake.
12. After moving the baking sheets, continue baking for another 12 to 15 minutes, or until the edges are crisp and brown.
13. Take them out of the oven, then carefully separate them into irregularly shaped crackers.
14. Return the unfinished crackers to the oven and bake them for an additional 5 to 10 minutes if necessary.

**Nutritional Information** (per serving)
48 Calories
3 grams of fat
5 grams of carbs
2 grams of protein

**Nutritional Profile:**
Diabetes-appropriate, heart-healthy, low-calorie, low-carbohydrate, low-fat, low-sodium, dairy-free, egg-free, nut-free, vegan, vegetarian

**Tips:**

To save for later: Store crackers in an airtight container for up to a week.

**No. 22: Air Fryer Sweet Potato Fries**

Sweet potato fries that have been air-fried are crisp, soft, and subtly sweet. They are a healthier alternative when you want crunchy potatoes because they are also created with less fat than standard fries. Try thyme, oregano, paprika, or garlic as a substitute if the cinnamon-pepper spice is too overpowering.

**Preparation Time:** 10 Minutes

**Extra Time:** 10 Minutes

**Overall Time:** 20 Minutes

**Portions:** 4

**Produced:** 4 servings

**Ingredients:**

- Olive oil, 1 tablespoon
- 1/4 teaspoon powdered cinnamon 1/4 teaspoon cayenne pepper 1/4 teaspoon sea salt
- 2 medium sweet potatoes, peeled and chopped into 1/4-inch sticks

**Directions:**

1. Apply cooking spray sparingly to a basket for an air fryer.
2. In a large bowl, mix the oil, cinnamon, cayenne, salt, and pepper.
3. Sweet potatoes should be added and thoroughly coated.
4. Put the sweet potatoes in the prepared basket in a single layer.
5. Cook for 14 minutes, flipping halfway through, at 400 degrees Fahren-

heit until golden and crispy.

6. Transfer the fries to a plate covered with paper towels to soak up any extra oil.

7. Serve right away.

**Nutritional Information** (per serving)

84 Calories

4 grams of fat

12 grams of carbs

1 gram of protein

**Nutritional Profile:**

Diabetes-appropriate, dairy-free, egg-free, gluten-free, nut-free, soy-free, heart-healthy, low-calorie, low-carbohydrate, low-sodium, vegan, vegetarian

**No. 23: Baked Zucchini Waffle Fries with Creamy Herb Dip**

These ranch-style waffle fries with crispy baked zucchini are a delicious snack, appetizer, or side dish. The creamy dipping sauce can be made with any kind of herb, such as chives, dill, tarragon, or parsley. The Old Bay in the breadcrumb coating on the zucchini mixes well with the sauce. You can use a mandoline or specialized waffle cutter to cut the waffle shape. If you don't want to mess with specific tools, you can choose to slice the zucchini.

**Preparation Time:** 25 Minutes

**Extra Time:** 20 Minutes

**Overall Time:** 45 Minutes

**Portions:** 6

**Produced:** 6 Servings

**Ingredients:**

- Nonstick cooking Spray
- Trim 1 12-ounce large zucchini; 3/4 cup fine, dry breadcrumbs; preferably whole-wheat
- Old Bay seasoning, 2 teaspoons
- 1/2 teaspoon divided into ground pepper
- 2 large eggs
- 1 tablespoon of water
- 1/4 cup plain, low-fat Greek yogurt
- Mayonnaise, 2 tablespoons
- Lemon juice, 1 tablespoon
- 1/2 teaspoon of garlic powder
- 1/8 teaspoon of salt
- 1/4 cup chopped herbs, such as parsley, tarragon, chives, and/or dill

**Equipment:** Mandoline or waffle cutter

**Directions:**

1. Set the oven's temperature to 425 F.
2. A large-rimmed baking sheet should have a wire rack on it. Spray the rack with cooking spray.
3. As the maker instructs, slice the zucchini into waffles using a handheld mandoline or waffle cutter.
4. In a pie pan, mix the breadcrumbs, Old Bay, and 1/4 teaspoon pepper.
5. In a second pie pan, combine eggs and water.
6. Before covering both sides with the breadcrumb mixture, dip the zucchini slices into the egg mixture.
7. On the ready rack, arrange the coated zucchini. Spray some frying oil on it. Bake for 25 to 30 minutes, until crisp and golden.
8. While that is going on, combine the yogurt, mayonnaise, lemon juice, garlic powder, salt, and a final 1/4 teaspoon of pepper in a small bowl.

9. The zucchini fries should be served with the herb mixture.

**Nutritional Information** (per serving)

84 Calories

5 grams of fat

7 grams of carbs

4 grams of protein

**Nutritional Profile:**

Diabetes-appropriate, heart-healthy, low-calorie, low-carbohydrate, low-sodium, nut-free, soy-free, vegetarian

## No. 24: Vegan Chocolate-Dipped Frozen Banana Bites

These little frozen pieces of vegan chocolate, peanut butter, and banana create the ideal low-calorie snack or quick dessert. Make a few extras of these banana bites and freeze them so you'll have them on hand when you're craving something sweet.

**Preparation Time:** 30 Minutes

**Extra Time:** 2 Hours

**Overall Time:** 2 Hours, 30 Minutes

**Portions:** 24

**Produced:** 24 Banana bites

**Ingredients:**

- 3 large bananas
- 1/4 cup natural peanut butter, either smooth or chunky

- 3/4 cup of vegan chocolate chips

**Directions:**

1. Each peeled banana should be split lengthwise.
2. Spread peanut butter on each half.
3. Combine the banana halves to create banana "sandwiches."
4. Each "sandwich" of bananas should have eight rounds.
5. Place the frozen banana pieces on a baking sheet or tray that has been lined with parchment paper or wax paper, and freeze for at least two hours or overnight.
6. In a microwave-safe bowl, add the chocolate chips. Microwave on high for 1 to 1 1/2 minutes, stirring after each 15-second interval, until completely melted.
7. Each frozen banana bite is coated with chocolate on one half.
8. Wait until the chocolate has set before serving.
9. If it is not consumed right away, put it back in the freezer.

**Nutritional Information** (per serving)
58 Calories
3 grams of fat
8 grams of carbs
1 gram of protein

**Nutritional Profile:**
Diabetes-appropriate, dairy-free, egg-free, gluten-free, soy-free, heart-healthy, low-calorie, low-carbohydrate, low-fat, low added sugars, vegan, vegetarian

**Tips:**

To save for later: Store in the freezer in a covered container for up to 1 month. Eat directly from the freezer.

## No. 25: Citrus Salsa with Baked Chips

This spicy salsa, made with tomatoes and citrus, is perfect for cold munching.

**Preparation Time:** 20 Minutes

**Extra Time:** 10 Minutes

**Overall Time:** 30 Minutes

**Portions:** 8

**Produced:** 8 Servings

**Ingredients:**

- 4 tortillas, corn
- Cooking spray, nonstick
- 1 cup of chopped citrus fruit segments (such as kumquats, tangerines, blood oranges, clementines, grapefruit, oranges, and/or clementines)
- 1/2 cup tomato, chopped
- 1/2 cup of cucumbers, chopped
- 2 tablespoons of green onion, chopped
- 2 tablespoons of fresh cilantro, chopped
- 1/4 teaspoon of red pepper flakes
- 1/4 teaspoon of salt

**Directions:**

1. Set the oven to 400 degrees Fahrenheit.
2. Spray nonstick frying spray on one side of each tortilla to prepare the chips.
3. Make eight wedges out of each tortilla.

4. Place on a parchment-paper-lined baking sheet.
5. Bake for 8 to 10 minutes, until crisp and gently browned. Cool.
6. To make the salsa, combine the citrus fruit, tomato, cucumber, green onion, cilantro, salt, and crushed red pepper in a small bowl.

**Nutritional Information** (per serving)

41 Calories

9 grams of carbs

1 gram of protein

**Nutritional Profile:**

Diabetes-appropriate, dairy-free, egg-free, gluten-free, nut-free, soy-free, heart-healthy, low-calorie, low-carbohydrate, vegan, vegetarian

**Tips:**

To prepare ahead of time: Prepare chips as directed in Step 1. Place chips in an airtight container, cover, and store at room temperature for up to 3 days. Prepare salsa as directed in Step 2. Spoon salsa into an airtight container, cover it and store it in the refrigerator for up to 4 hours.

**No. 26: Pumpkin Oat Mini Muffins**

Oats and chocolate chips are plentiful in these gluten-free pumpkin muffins. Additionally, since the entire recipe for these tiny pumpkin muffins is produced in the blender, cleanup is a breeze. Make 12 regular-sized muffins instead by baking them for 18 to 20 minutes and cooling them in the pan for 10 minutes before removing them from the pan.

**Preparation Time:** 15 Minutes

**Extra Time:** 30 Minutes

**Overall Time:** 45 Minutes

**Portions:** 24

**Produced:** 24 Mini muffins

**Ingredients:**

- Rolling oats, 1-1/2 cups (see tips below)
- 1 teaspoon of baking powder
- Pumpkin pie spice, 1 teaspoon
- 1/4 teaspoon of baking soda
- A pinch of of salt
- 2 large eggs
- 1 cup of pureed, unseasoned pumpkin
- 3/4 packed cups of dark brown sugar
- 3 tablespoons of canola or grapeseed oil
- Vanilla extract, 1 teaspoon
- 1/3 cup dried cranberries or tiny chocolate chips

**Directions:**

1. Set the oven to 350 degrees Fahrenheit.
2. Spray some cooking oil in a 24-cup mini muffin pan.
3. In a blender, pulse oats until they are powdered.
4. Salt, baking soda, pumpkin pie spice, and baking powder should all be added; pulse once or twice to combine.
5. Blend till smooth after adding the eggs, pumpkin, brown sugar, oil, and vanilla.
6. Add the chocolate (or cranberry) chips.
7. Fill the muffin cups two-thirds of the way full.
8. Bake the muffins for 15 to 17 minutes, or until a toothpick inserted in the center comes out clean.

9. After 5 minutes on a wire rack in the pan, turn it out to finish cooling.

**Nutritional Information** (per serving)

82 Calories

3 grams of fat

13 grams of carbs

1 gram of protein

**Nutritional Profile:**

Diabetes-appropriate, heart-healthy, nut-free, soy-free, low-calorie, low-carbohydrate, low-fat, and low-sodium

**Tips:** A word of advice: Because oats are frequently contaminated with wheat and barley, those who have celiac disease or gluten sensitivity should only use oats that are marked "gluten-free."

**No. 27: Blueberry Muffin Bars**

The abundance of supersized muffins makes portion control difficult. These blueberry muffin bars let you enjoy the flavors of a blueberry muffin while keeping track of your food intake with ease.

**Preparation Time:** 25 Minutes

**Extra Time:** 35 Minutes

**Overall Time:** 1 Hour

**Portions:** 32

**Produced:** 32 Servings

**Ingredients:**

- Cooking spray, nonstick
- Quick-cooking rolled oats, 1-3/4 cups
- 3/4 cup packed brown sugar (see tips below) 3/4 cup all-purpose flour and 3/4 cup whole wheat flour
- 1 teaspoon of apple pie spice
- 1 stick of light butter, or 1/2 cup
- 1/2 cup of finely chopped almond slivers
- 1 cup of blueberry preserves without sugar
- 1/2 teaspoon of almond extract

## Directions:

1. Set the oven to 350 degrees Fahrenheit.
2. To line a 13 x 9 x 2-inch baking pan, fold aluminum foil over the pan's edges.
3. Cooking Spray the foil lightly, then set it aside.
4. Oats, all-purpose flour, whole wheat flour, brown sugar, and apple pie spice should all be combined in a big bowl.
5. Add the light butter and pulse with a pastry blender until the mixture resembles a coarse meal.
6. Almonds should be mixed into 3/4 cup of the crumb mixture before being transferred.
7. Set aside.
8. The bottom of the prepared pan should be covered with the leftover crumb mixture.
9. For 10 minutes, bake.
10. Combine the preserves and almond essence in a small bowl.
11. Spread preserves evenly over the crust with care.
12. Sprinkle the remaining crumb mixture on top and lightly press.
13. The top should be faintly browned after 20 to 25 minutes of baking.
14. On a wire rack, let the pan completely cool.
15. Using foil, remove from pan and cut into bars.
16. To keep the remaining bars, wrap them in foil.

**Nutritional Information** (per serving)

89 Calories

12 grams of fat

15 grams of carbs

2 grams of protein

**Nutritional Profile:**

Diabetes-appropriate, egg-free, soy-free, heart-healthy, low-calorie, low-carbohydrate, low-sodium, vegetarian

**Tips:**

In this recipe, it is not recommended to substitute white sugar for brown sugar.

**No. 28: Cranberry Crumble Bars**

These bars of cranberry and orange freeze wonderfully. To ensure that you always have a healthy dessert available when company visits, prepare a batch on a free afternoon and store it in the freezer.

**Preparation Time:** 25 Minutes

**Extra Time:** 55 Minutes

**Overall Time:** 1 Hour, 20 Minutes

**Portions:** 15

**Produced:** 15 Bars

**Ingredients:**

## For the filling:

- 2 cups of cranberries 1/2 an orange's juice and zest (see tips below)
- 6 tablespoons of sugar, granulated
- 1-1/2 tablespoons of cornstarch
- Ground cinnamon, 1/4 teaspoon, and 2 teaspoons of almond extract

## For the crust:

- Half a cup of all-purpose flour
- 1/2 cup granulated sugar and 1-1/2 cups almond flour
- 1 teaspoon of baking powder
- 1/4 teaspoon each of salt and powdered nutmeg
- 1/2 orange's zest
- 4 tablespoons diced, cold, unsalted butter
- 2 large egg whites
- Vanilla extract, 1-1/2 teaspoons
- 2 teaspoons of powdered sugar (optional)

## Directions:

1. Set the oven to 375 degrees Fahrenheit.
2. Using parchment paper, line a 9 x 13-inch baking sheet, allowing some overhang on the long edges. (The extra will assist you in removing the bars.)
3. Cranberries, orange zest, orange juice, 6 tablespoons of granulated sugar, cornstarch, almond essence, and cinnamon should be mixed in a small bowl to make the filling. Place aside.
4. All-purpose flour, almond flour, 1/2 cup granulated sugar, baking powder, salt, nutmeg, and orange zest should be combined in a medium bowl to make the crust.
5. Once the pieces are flattened and the mixture is crumbly and resembles sand, work butter into the mixture by pinching and rubbing with your

hands.

6. In a small dish, whisk the egg whites and vanilla using a fork.
7. Pour into the flour mixture, then, using a fork, scoop up through the middle and down from the edges until all of the whites have been thoroughly combined.
8. Half of the mixture should be set aside.
9. To create a bottom crust, press the remaining mixture into the prepared baking pan.
10. The cranberry sauce should be stirred briefly before being poured over the crust and baked.
11. Top with the crust mixture that was set aside.
12. About 40 minutes of baking time is required to lightly brown the top.
13. The bars should cool in the pan for 15 minutes before being transferred to a wire rack.
14. By using its long edges, you can lift the parchment and place it on a cutting board for removal. 15 bars should be cut with a sharp knife.
15. Complete cooling.
16. If desired, garnish the food with powdered sugar before serving.

**Equipment:** 9 x 13-inch baking pan, parchment paper

**Nutritional Information** (per serving)
199 Calories
9 grams of fat
27 grams of carbs
4 grams of protein

**Nutritional Profile:**
Diabetes-appropriate, heart-healthy, low-calorie, low-sodium, soy-free, vegetarian

**Tips:**

Don't skip the zest, even if you don't have a microplane or zester. Instead, remove only the orange portion of the fruit's skin using a vegetable peeler. Discard as much of the white pith as you can. After that, stack the strips and finely chop them with a knife.

Use Splenda Sugar Blend as a sugar substitute when baking. Use the equivalent of 6 TBSP for the filling and ½ cup for the crust as directed on the packaging. Leave out the sugary garnish.

Making ahead: Allow the bars to cool completely before layering them between parchment-lined sheets in a container or sealable bag. Freeze for up to four months or refrigerate for up to a day. Place on a dish and let sit for an hour to thaw before serving frozen.

**No. 29: Almond and Pear Rose Tarts**

These lovely two-bite almond and pear tarts are ideal for party platters, especially in the autumn when pears are in season. Thinly slicing the pears allows you to roll the tarts up more cleanly, creating a bakery-worthy look. If you have a mandoline, now is the time to use it. Cold puff pastry is essential for achieving wonderfully flaky results.

Do you want to make this simple, healthful dessert gluten-free? Simply substitute gluten-free puff pastry, which can be purchased in the frozen section of most grocery stores. Don't forget to roll it out with an all-purpose gluten-free flour blend!

**Preparation Time:** 35 Minutes

**Extra Time:** 30 Minutes

**Overall Time:** 1 Hour, 5 Minutes

**Portions:** 10

**Produced:** 10 Tarts

**Ingredients:**

- Sugar, 2 teaspoons
- 1/4 teaspoon each of ground cinnamon and cardamom
- A dash of salt
- 2 medium-sized red pears, cut into 4 cups
- All-purpose flour for rolling and dusting surfaces
- 1 sheet of thawed puff pastry from the freezer, chilled
- Almond paste, 3 tablespoons

**Directions:**

1. Set the oven to 400 degrees Fahrenheit.
2. Spray cooking spray in a 12-cup muffin pan sparingly.
3. In a large bowl, mix the sugar, cardamom, cinnamon, and salt.
4. Pears should be added and coated.
5. Add flour to a tidy work surface.
6. The chilled, thawed puff pastry should be unfolded and rolled out to a 10-inch square.
7. Make 1-inch-wide strips.
8. Roll the almond paste into a 5-by-8-inch rectangle and re-dust the surface.
9. Measure 1/2 inch by 8 inches and cut into 10 strips.
10. Lay pears lengthwise on top of each pastry strip, leaving a 1-inch space at each end, then top each with an almond strip.
11. When rolling the pastry into a coil, begin at a short edge and gently tuck the extra pastry under the cut side of the pears.
12. Fill the muffin tray that has been prepared.
13. The tin should be frozen for five minutes.

14. Bake the tarts for 20 to 25 minutes, or until golden brown.
15. Before serving, let it cool for 5 minutes.

**Equipment:** Muffin tin with 12 (½ cup) cups

**Nutritional Information** (per serving)
   186 Calories
   11 grams of fat
   20 grams of carbs
   3 grams of protein

**Nutritional Profile:**
   Diabetes-appropriate, heart-healthy, dairy-free, egg-free, low in added sugars, low in sodium, vegetarian

**Tips:**

To prepare ahead of time: Store in the refrigerator for up to 1 day. Before serving, reheat the dish slightly.

**No. 30: Vanilla Cake**

This lightened-up cake tastes like actual vanilla beans, but it's still sweet and wonderful on its own or topped with your favorite icing.

**Preparation Time:** 25 Minutes

**Extra Time:** 35 Minutes

**Overall Time:** 1 Hour

**Portions:** 16

**Produced:** 16 Servings

**Ingredients:**

- Fat-free milk, 3/4 cup
- 1/4 cup of butter
- 3 eggs, room temperature, 1 vanilla bean,
- Sugar, 1-1/4 cups (see tips below)
- All-purpose flour, 1-1/2 cups
- Baking powder, 1-1/2 teaspoons
- 1/4 teaspoon of salt
- Vanilla extract, 1-1/2 teaspoons

**Directions:**

1. Butter and milk are combined in a small saucepan.
2. Split the vanilla bean in half lengthwise using a small, precise knife.
3. Seeds from the halves should be scraped into the milk mixture.
4. Half a vanilla bean should be added to the pot.
5. Stirring regularly, heat over medium heat (do not boil) until butter is melted and milk is steaming. Get rid of the heat.
6. Set the oven to 350 degrees Fahrenheit.
7. Meanwhile, lightly grease two 8-inch round cake pans' bottoms.
8. Pans should be greased and lightly dusted with flour before lining the bottoms with parchment or waxed paper.
9. Eggs should be beaten on high speed in a big bowl for about 4 minutes, or until thick and light yellow.
10. Add sugar gradually while beating for 4 to 5 minutes at medium speed, or until the mixture is light and fluffy.
11. Add salt, baking soda, and flour.
12. Just until blended, beat on low to medium.
13. Take out and discard the vanilla bean halves from the milk mixture.
14. Mix the milk mixture and vanilla essence into the batter after adding

them. Spread out the batter evenly among the prepared pans.
15. 25 minutes should be allotted for baking, or until a toothpick inserted close to the middle comes out clean.
16. For 10 minutes, the cake layers should cool in the pans.
17. Layers can be taken out of pans and cooled on wire racks.

**Nutritional Information** (per serving)
148 Calories
4 grams of fat
26 grams of carbs
3 grams of protein

**Nutritional Profile:**
Diabetes-appropriate, heart-healthy, low-calorie, low-sodium, nut-free, soy-free, vegetarian

**Tips:**

If you must use a sugar replacement, use Splenda (R) Sugar Blend. To use the product amount equivalent to 1-1/4 cups of sugar, follow the package recommendations. Nutritional Information Per Serving with Substitute: Same as above, except 125 calories and 17 grams of carbohydrates (8 grams of sugars).

**In Summary**

This is far from a comprehensive list of type 2 diabetes dessert recipes. I've experimented with these recipes many times over the years, mixing and matching, and I encourage you to do the same. Make these dessert recipes to fit your specific needs.

In addition, I recommend that you use these dessert recipes to plan your meals with the planners that I have included. Enjoy!

# 10

# Meal Planners, Shopping & Inventory Lists.

Meal preparation provides us with numerous unexpected rewards. This includes reaching our exercise objectives, increasing our health, decreasing waste, and saving a significant amount of time and money. With that, I strongly advise you to use these handy meal planners to help you with that!

These basic planners are excellent quality and printable, allowing you to plan your meal ideas. With these easy-to-use planners, you may finally have your ideal organized meal planner in the palm of your hands without spending any money at the store.

Included as well is a shopping list planner, so you can stay organized and on top of your grocery shopping. This easy-to-use planner allows you to make a shopping list in minutes, with spaces for categorizing goods and recording quantities. With this must-have shopping list planner, grocery shopping will be a breeze!

Meal planners, shopping lists, and inventory lists.

# MEAL PLANNER

| MONTH | | WEEK | |

|  | BREAKFAST | LUNCH | DINNER | DESSERT |
|---|---|---|---|---|
| MON | | | | |
| TUES | | | | |
| WED | | | | |
| THUR | | | | |
| FRI | | | | |
| SAT | | | | |
| SUN | | | | |

# MEAL PLANNER

| MONTH | | WEEK | |

| | BREAKFAST | LUNCH | DINNER | DESSERT |
|------|-----------|-------|--------|---------|
| MON | | | | |
| TUES | | | | |
| WED | | | | |
| THUR | | | | |
| FRI | | | | |
| SAT | | | | |
| SUN | | | | |

# MEAL PLANNER

| MONTH | | WEEK | |

| | BREAKFAST | LUNCH | DINNER | DESSERT |
|---|---|---|---|---|
| MON | | | | |
| TUES | | | | |
| WED | | | | |
| THUR | | | | |
| FRI | | | | |
| SAT | | | | |
| SUN | | | | |

253

# MEAL PLANNER

| MONTH | | | WEEK | |
|---|---|---|---|---|

| | BREAKFAST | LUNCH | DINNER | DESSERT |
|---|---|---|---|---|
| MON | | | | |
| TUES | | | | |
| WED | | | | |
| THUR | | | | |
| FRI | | | | |
| SAT | | | | |
| SUN | | | | |

# MEAL PLANNER

| MONTH | | WEEK | |

|  | BREAKFAST | LUNCH | DINNER | DESSERT |
|---|---|---|---|---|
| MON | | | | |
| TUES | | | | |
| WED | | | | |
| THUR | | | | |
| FRI | | | | |
| SAT | | | | |
| SUN | | | | |

255

# MEAL PLANNER

| MONTH | | WEEK | |
|---|---|---|---|

| | BREAKFAST | LUNCH | DINNER | DESSERT |
|---|---|---|---|---|
| MON | | | | |
| TUES | | | | |
| WED | | | | |
| THUR | | | | |
| FRI | | | | |
| SAT | | | | |
| SUN | | | | |

MEAL PLANNERS, SHOPPING & INVENTORY LISTS.

## MONTHLY PLANNER    JAN FEB MAR APR MAY JUN JUL AUG SEP OCT NOV DEC

| MONDAY | TUESDAY | WEDNESDAY | THURSDAY | FRIDAY | SATURDAY | SUNDAY |
|---|---|---|---|---|---|---|
|  |  |  |  |  |  |  |
|  |  |  |  |  |  |  |
|  |  |  |  |  |  |  |
|  |  |  |  |  |  |  |
|  |  |  |  |  |  |  |

Notes:

## MONTHLY PLANNER     JAN FEB MAR APR MAY JUN JUL AUG SEP OCT NOV DEC

| MONDAY | TUESDAY | WEDNESDAY | THURSDAY | FRIDAY | SATURDAY | SUNDAY |
|--------|---------|-----------|----------|--------|----------|--------|
|        |         |           |          |        |          |        |
|        |         |           |          |        |          |        |
|        |         |           |          |        |          |        |
|        |         |           |          |        |          |        |
|        |         |           |          |        |          |        |

Notes:

MEAL PLANNERS, SHOPPING & INVENTORY LISTS.

## MONTHLY PLANNER     JAN FEB MAR APR MAY JUN JUL AUG SEP OCT NOV DEC

| MONDAY | TUESDAY | WEDNESDAY | THURSDAY | FRIDAY | SATURDAY | SUNDAY |
|--------|---------|-----------|----------|--------|----------|--------|
|        |         |           |          |        |          |        |
|        |         |           |          |        |          |        |
|        |         |           |          |        |          |        |
|        |         |           |          |        |          |        |
|        |         |           |          |        |          |        |

Notes:

**MONTHLY PLANNER**   JAN FEB MAR APR MAY JUN JUL AUG SEP OCT NOV DEC

| MONDAY | TUESDAY | WEDNESDAY | THURSDAY | FRIDAY | SATURDAY | SUNDAY |
|---|---|---|---|---|---|---|
|  |  |  |  |  |  |  |
|  |  |  |  |  |  |  |
|  |  |  |  |  |  |  |
|  |  |  |  |  |  |  |
|  |  |  |  |  |  |  |

Notes:

MEAL PLANNERS, SHOPPING & INVENTORY LISTS.

**MONTHLY PLANNER**     JAN FEB MAR APR MAY JUN JUL AUG SEP OCT NOV DEC

| MONDAY | TUESDAY | WEDNESDAY | THURSDAY | FRIDAY | SATURDAY | SUNDAY |
|---|---|---|---|---|---|---|
| | | | | | | |
| | | | | | | |
| | | | | | | |
| | | | | | | |
| | | | | | | |

Notes:

261

**MONTHLY PLANNER**    JAN FEB MAR APR MAY JUN JUL AUG SEP OCT NOV DEC

| MONDAY | TUESDAY | WEDNESDAY | THURSDAY | FRIDAY | SATURDAY | SUNDAY |
|--------|---------|-----------|----------|--------|----------|--------|
|        |         |           |          |        |          |        |
|        |         |           |          |        |          |        |
|        |         |           |          |        |          |        |
|        |         |           |          |        |          |        |
|        |         |           |          |        |          |        |

Notes:

MEAL PLANNERS, SHOPPING & INVENTORY LISTS.

## MONTHLY PLANNER     JAN FEB MAR APR MAY JUN JUL AUG SEP OCT NOV DEC

| MONDAY | TUESDAY | WEDNESDAY | THURSDAY | FRIDAY | SATURDAY | SUNDAY |
|---|---|---|---|---|---|---|
|  |  |  |  |  |  |  |
|  |  |  |  |  |  |  |
|  |  |  |  |  |  |  |
|  |  |  |  |  |  |  |
|  |  |  |  |  |  |  |

Notes:

## MONTHLY PLANNER   JAN FEB MAR APR MAY JUN JUL AUG SEP OCT NOV DEC

| MONDAY | TUESDAY | WEDNESDAY | THURSDAY | FRIDAY | SATURDAY | SUNDAY |
|---|---|---|---|---|---|---|
| | | | | | | |
| | | | | | | |
| | | | | | | |
| | | | | | | |
| | | | | | | |

Notes:

MEAL PLANNERS, SHOPPING & INVENTORY LISTS.

## MONTHLY PLANNER    JAN FEB MAR APR MAY JUN JUL AUG SEP OCT NOV DEC

| MONDAY | TUESDAY | WEDNESDAY | THURSDAY | FRIDAY | SATURDAY | SUNDAY |
|--------|---------|-----------|----------|--------|----------|--------|
|        |         |           |          |        |          |        |
|        |         |           |          |        |          |        |
|        |         |           |          |        |          |        |
|        |         |           |          |        |          |        |
|        |         |           |          |        |          |        |

Notes:

## MONTHLY PLANNER

JAN FEB MAR APR MAY JUN JUL AUG SEP OCT NOV DEC

| MONDAY | TUESDAY | WEDNESDAY | THURSDAY | FRIDAY | SATURDAY | SUNDAY |
|--------|---------|-----------|----------|--------|----------|--------|
|        |         |           |          |        |          |        |
|        |         |           |          |        |          |        |
|        |         |           |          |        |          |        |
|        |         |           |          |        |          |        |
|        |         |           |          |        |          |        |

Notes:

## MONTHLY PLANNER    JAN FEB MAR APR MAY JUN JUL AUG SEP OCT NOV DEC

| MONDAY | TUESDAY | WEDNESDAY | THURSDAY | FRIDAY | SATURDAY | SUNDAY |
|--------|---------|-----------|----------|--------|----------|--------|
|        |         |           |          |        |          |        |
|        |         |           |          |        |          |        |
|        |         |           |          |        |          |        |
|        |         |           |          |        |          |        |
|        |         |           |          |        |          |        |

Notes:

**MONTHLY PLANNER**     JAN FEB MAR APR MAY JUN JUL AUG SEP OCT NOV DEC

| MONDAY | TUESDAY | WEDNESDAY | THURSDAY | FRIDAY | SATURDAY | SUNDAY |
|--------|---------|-----------|----------|--------|----------|--------|
|        |         |           |          |        |          |        |
|        |         |           |          |        |          |        |
|        |         |           |          |        |          |        |
|        |         |           |          |        |          |        |
|        |         |           |          |        |          |        |

Notes:

# WEEKLY
# SHOPPING LIST

### WEEK - 1

| FROZEN | MEAT | BAKERY | FRUIT | SNACK |
|--------|------|--------|-------|-------|
|        |      |        |       |       |

### WEEK - 2

| FROZEN | MEAT | BAKERY | FRUIT | SNACK |
|--------|------|--------|-------|-------|
|        |      |        |       |       |

### WEEK - 3

| FROZEN | MEAT | BAKERY | FRUIT | SNACK |
|--------|------|--------|-------|-------|
|        |      |        |       |       |

### WEEK - 4

| FROZEN | MEAT | BAKERY | FRUIT | SNACK |
|--------|------|--------|-------|-------|
|        |      |        |       |       |

### WEEK - 5

| FROZEN | MEAT | BAKERY | FRUIT | SNACK |
|--------|------|--------|-------|-------|
|        |      |        |       |       |

NOTES_____

# WEEKLY
# SHOPPING LIST

**WEEK - 1**

| FROZEN | MEAT | BAKERY | FRUIT | SNACK |
|--------|------|--------|-------|-------|
|        |      |        |       |       |

**WEEK - 2**

| FROZEN | MEAT | BAKERY | FRUIT | SNACK |
|--------|------|--------|-------|-------|
|        |      |        |       |       |

**WEEK - 3**

| FROZEN | MEAT | BAKERY | FRUIT | SNACK |
|--------|------|--------|-------|-------|
|        |      |        |       |       |

**WEEK - 4**

| FROZEN | MEAT | BAKERY | FRUIT | SNACK |
|--------|------|--------|-------|-------|
|        |      |        |       |       |

**WEEK - 5**

| FROZEN | MEAT | BAKERY | FRUIT | SNACK |
|--------|------|--------|-------|-------|
|        |      |        |       |       |

NOTES

# WEEKLY
# SHOPPING LIST

**WEEK - 1**

| FROZEN | MEAT | BAKERY | FRUIT | SNACK |
|--------|------|--------|-------|-------|
|        |      |        |       |       |

**WEEK - 2**

| FROZEN | MEAT | BAKERY | FRUIT | SNACK |
|--------|------|--------|-------|-------|
|        |      |        |       |       |

**WEEK - 3**

| FROZEN | MEAT | BAKERY | FRUIT | SNACK |
|--------|------|--------|-------|-------|
|        |      |        |       |       |

**WEEK - 4**

| FROZEN | MEAT | BAKERY | FRUIT | SNACK |
|--------|------|--------|-------|-------|
|        |      |        |       |       |

**WEEK - 5**

| FROZEN | MEAT | BAKERY | FRUIT | SNACK |
|--------|------|--------|-------|-------|
|        |      |        |       |       |

NOTES_____

271

# WEEKLY
# SHOPPING LIST

---

WEEK – 1

| FROZEN | MEAT | BAKERY | FRUIT | SNACK |
|--------|------|--------|-------|-------|
|        |      |        |       |       |

WEEK – 2

| FROZEN | MEAT | BAKERY | FRUIT | SNACK |
|--------|------|--------|-------|-------|
|        |      |        |       |       |

WEEK – 3

| FROZEN | MEAT | BAKERY | FRUIT | SNACK |
|--------|------|--------|-------|-------|
|        |      |        |       |       |

WEEK – 4

| FROZEN | MEAT | BAKERY | FRUIT | SNACK |
|--------|------|--------|-------|-------|
|        |      |        |       |       |

WEEK – 5

| FROZEN | MEAT | BAKERY | FRUIT | SNACK |
|--------|------|--------|-------|-------|
|        |      |        |       |       |

NOTES_____

# List Of Meals

**MY FOOD JOURNAL**

| MONDAY | | TUESDAY | |
|---|---|---|---|
| | | | |
| CALORIES : | CARBS : | CALORIES : | CARBS : |

| WEDNESDAY | | THURSDAY | |
|---|---|---|---|
| | | | |
| CALORIES : | CARBS : | CALORIES : | CARBS : |

| FRIDAY | | SATURDAY | |
|---|---|---|---|
| | | | |
| CALORIES : | CARBS : | CALORIES : | CARBS : |

NOTES: _____

_____

# List Of Meals

**MY FOOD JOURNAL**

| MONDAY | | TUESDAY | |
|---|---|---|---|
| | | | |
| CALORIES : | CARBS : | CALORIES : | CARBS : |

| WEDNESDAY | | THURSDAY | |
|---|---|---|---|
| | | | |
| CALORIES : | CARBS : | CALORIES : | CARBS : |

| FRIDAY | | SATURDAY | |
|---|---|---|---|
| | | | |
| CALORIES : | CARBS : | CALORIES : | CARBS : |

NOTES: _____

_____

# List Of Meals

## MY FOOD JOURNAL

| MONDAY | | TUESDAY | |
|---|---|---|---|
| | | | |
| CALORIES : | CARBS : | CALORIES : | CARBS : |

| WEDNESDAY | | THURSDAY | |
|---|---|---|---|
| | | | |
| CALORIES : | CARBS : | CALORIES : | CARBS : |

| FRIDAY | | SATURDAY | |
|---|---|---|---|
| | | | |
| CALORIES : | CARBS : | CALORIES : | CARBS : |

NOTES: _____

_____

# List Of Meals

**MY FOOD JOURNAL**

| MONDAY | | TUESDAY | |
|---|---|---|---|
| | | | |
| CALORIES : | CARBS : | CALORIES : | CARBS : |

| WEDNESDAY | | THURSDAY | |
|---|---|---|---|
| | | | |
| CALORIES : | CARBS : | CALORIES : | CARBS : |

| FRIDAY | | SATURDAY | |
|---|---|---|---|
| | | | |
| CALORIES : | CARBS : | CALORIES : | CARBS : |

NOTES: _____

_____

# KITCHEN INVENTORY

| MEAT | FRUIT | VEGETABLES |
|------|-------|------------|
|      |       |            |
|      |       |            |
|      |       |            |
|      |       |            |
|      |       |            |
|      |       |            |
|      |       |            |

| DRY, CANNED FOODS | MISCELLANEOUS |
|-------------------|---------------|
|                   |               |
|                   |               |
|                   |               |
|                   |               |
|                   |               |
|                   |               |
|                   |               |

NOTES

# KITCHEN INVENTORY

| MEAT | FRUIT | VEGETABLES |
| --- | --- | --- |
|  |  |  |
|  |  |  |
|  |  |  |
|  |  |  |
|  |  |  |
|  |  |  |
|  |  |  |
|  |  |  |
|  |  |  |

| DRY, CANNED FOODS | MISCELLANEOUS |
| --- | --- |
|  |  |
|  |  |
|  |  |
|  |  |
|  |  |
|  |  |
|  |  |
|  |  |
|  |  |

NOTES

# KITCHEN INVENTORY

| MEAT | FRUIT | VEGETABLES |
|------|-------|------------|
|      |       |            |
|      |       |            |
|      |       |            |
|      |       |            |
|      |       |            |
|      |       |            |
|      |       |            |
|      |       |            |

| DRY, CANNED FOODS | MISCELLANEOUS |
|-------------------|---------------|
|                   |               |
|                   |               |
|                   |               |
|                   |               |
|                   |               |
|                   |               |
|                   |               |

NOTES

# KITCHEN INVENTORY

| MEAT | FRUIT | VEGETABLES |
| --- | --- | --- |
| | | |
| | | |
| | | |
| | | |
| | | |
| | | |
| | | |

| DRY, CANNED FOODS | MISCELLANEOUS |
| --- | --- |
| | |
| | |
| | |
| | |
| | |
| | |
| | |

NOTES

# 11

# Conclusion

I n conclusion, this type 2 diabetic cookbook is an excellent way to begin making your own food. It's an excellent choice for beginners because it lets you control and manage your type 2 diabetes, which can be difficult at first. With this cookbook, you can tailor the recipes to your specific needs, and it's so nice to have it on hand when you need it. Diabetic cookbooks are also a terrific way to make the most of a circumstance that most people did not choose: diabetes. Furthermore, these diabetic recipes are an excellent way to improve your general health and well-being. Also, cooking with this type 2 diabetes cookbook is an enjoyable and satisfying way to spend your time indoors. It's a terrific opportunity to get some exercise and enjoy the fresh scents while controlling your type 2 diabetes. In addition, the sense of success you'll feel when you bite into cuisine created from these type 2 diabetes recipes is simply unparalleled. So, whether you're a beginner or a seasoned chef, this type 2 diabetes cookbook is an excellent choice to explore. You can create lovely meals that will give you fresh, organic meals all year with a little forethought, a few ingredients, and a little TLC, and you're done! So don't be afraid to try it; you'll be surprised at what you can cook! I hope that after reading this cookbook, you feel confident in your ability to prepare your own diabetic meals. I also hope that this cookbook has helped you get started with cooking your own diabetic meals. I believe that by following the directions, tips, and tricks in this cookbook, you will be able to create wonderful dishes that will help you control and manage your type 2 diabetes. If you loved this cookbook and found it useful, I would really appreciate it if you could write a favorable review on Amazon. Your input is valuable to me and assists other readers in discovering the book. Good luck with your cooking!

# 12

# Resources

G *oogle*. (n.d.-b). https://www.google.ca/

*Type 2 symptoms*. (n.d.). DiabetesCanadaWebsite. https://www.diabetes.ca/about-diabetes/type-2/symptoms

*American Diabetes Association | Research, Education, Advocacy*. (n.d.). https://diabetes.org/

*American Heart Association | To be a relentless force for a world of longer, healthier lives*. (n.d.). www.heart.org. https://www.heart.org/

*National Institutes of Health (NIH)*. (n.d.). National Institutes of Health (NIH). https://www.nih.gov/

*Practice Guidelines Resources | American Diabetes Association*. (n.d.). https://professional.diabetes.org/content-page/practice-guidelines-resources

*Who We are | Ludeman Family Center for Women's Health Research*. (n.d.). https://medschool.cuanschutz.edu/center-for-womens-health-research/about-us

Professional, C. C. M. (n.d.). *Diabetes*. Cleveland Clinic. https://my.cleveland clinic.org/health/diseases/7104-diabetes

*Type 2 diabetes: symptoms, causes, treatment.* (2006, December 31). WebMD. https://www.webmd.com/diabetes/type-2-diabetes

*Type 2 diabetes - Symptoms and causes - Mayo Clinic.* (2023, March 14). Mayo Clinic. https://www.mayoclinic.org/diseases-conditions/type-2-diabetes/sy mptoms-causes/syc-20351193

*EatingWell: Healthy Recipes, Healthy Eating.* (2022, September 28). EatingWell. https://www.eatingwell.com/

*Recipe ideas, product reviews, home decor inspiration, and beauty tips - good housekeeping.* (n.d.). Good Housekeeping. https://www.goodhousekeeping.c om/

*WeightWatchers Weight-Loss Program—Lose Weight and Keep it Off | WW USA.* (n.d.). https://www.weightwatchers.com/us/

Template.net. (2021, April 15). *Plan templates.* template.net. https://www.te mplate.net/business/plan-templates/

# About the Author

G.F. Quinn is an Indigenous Canadian author; he is Status First Nations from Alexander Reserve #134, and he was born in Lac La Biche, Alberta. grew up in Fort Mcmurray, Alberta, and for the past 25 years he has lived in the City of Champions, Edmonton, Alberta. He is a single father with one son; he also has four grandchildren. Loves pets, traveling, gardening, cooking, reading, and video games. He hopes to one day visit as many places as possible and experience the many cultures and breathtaking beauty of this beautiful world we all call home.

You can connect with me on:
- https://www.amazon.com/author/g.f.quinn
- https://twitter.com/GeorgeQ1972
- https://www.facebook.com/quinnpublishing.ca

# Also by G.F. Quinn

Throughout his childhood and adult life, G.F. Quinn has been involved in all areas of gardening. Using his extensive knowledge, practical methods, and his passion for gardening, he brings you this all inclusive book that will encourage you to understand raised bed gardens and ensure you're able to build and sustain your own.

Inside Raised-Bed Gardening for Beginners, you'll discover:

Five essential points for planning your gardening, including the pros and cons of the no-dig method. How to build your garden by using the right material, soil, and tools. The best way to plan your planting through spacing, watering, and crop rotation. Effective maintenance methods to improve your soil and ensure you secure a bountiful harvest. The costliest mistakes to avoid for your garden. PLUS: should you be using coffee grounds in your garden?

Every chapter in this book will bring you a step closer to having your own raised bed garden in just two days! No more worrying about wasting money, doing it wrong, or ending up with dead plants.

**Raised-Bed Gardening for Beginners: A Complete Guide To Growing A Healthy Organic Garden On A Budget, Using Tools And Materials You Probably Already Have!**

Are you a first-time gardener looking to grow a raised bed garden but you're not sure where to begin?

Do you aspire to build, grow, and sustain your garden but believe you need more guidance?

Have you been searching for a book that will not only answer your questions but empower you to build a successful and cost-effective garden?

Keep reading, this is the perfect book for you!

With a raised bed garden, you have more control over the health of your soil, you never have to deal with knee and back pain, and you're able to enjoy organic fresh produce throughout the year.

Although 55% of Americans are gardeners, not all of them can sustain their gardens for prolonged periods.

Are you ready to learn how?

Are you ready to get started with your garden?

Then grab Raised Bed-Gardening for Beginners now!

Made in the USA
Las Vegas, NV
14 January 2024

84383518R00162